I0450521

# THE CRIMINOLOGICAL SHERLOCK HOLMES

## An A to Z Guide to the Criminology of  Sherlock Holmes

### Kelvin Jones

### Cunning Crime Books

The Criminological Sherlock Holmes

First published 2015: cunningcrimebooks
www.cunningcrimebooks. co.uk

Author's note: Sections of this work have previously appeared in *Sherlock Holmes And CSI, The Sherlock Holmes Murder File ,A Sherlock Holmes Dictionary* and *Sherlock Holmes And Poisons.*

## INTRODUCTION

### Kelvin Jones

The most famous detective of all time, Sherlock Holmes, made his first public appearance in the December issue of Beeton's Christmas Annual for 1887. The story, A Study in Scarlet, was not an immediate success when it was reprinted by Ward Lock & Co. in the following year. That was unsurprising, however, for in August of that year the first of Jack the Ripper's many victims was added to the already high crime statistics of London. The appetite of the Victorian reading public enjoyed a full enough saturation of bloody murder and mayhem from the popular press of the day.

But perhaps there was another reason for the story's distinct lack of success. The detective within its pages was unlike any other. Arrogant, haughty, contemptuous of the official police-force but equipped with a rapier — like intelligence and all the resources of modern science, Sherlock Holmes reached his results by an apparently magical process.

To today's audience, the facts of forensic science are commonplace. But who, in 1888, had heard of fingerprinting? Certainly the London police did not accept it as a practical science. If they had done so, the mystery of Jack the Ripper would certainly not have remained thus. Handwriting identification was also in its infancy. An Austrian judge, Hans Gross, had realised its tremendous potential, but clearly the C.I.D.

3

(set up in 1877) did not think to analyse the three grim letters sent by the Ripper to the news agencies. In those days there was a distinct lack of co-operation between the medical profession and the police. All but one of the Ripper's victims were removed from the scene of the crime, their bodies stripped and washed ready for the mortuary, thus destroying valuable forensic evidence. This predicament is well reflected in A Study in Scarlet when, faced with the pathway outside No. 3 Lauriston Gardens, Brixton, Holmes remarks, 'If a herd of buffaloes had passed along there could not be a greater mess.'

The date of Holmes' debut (1881) is an important one to the student of criminology. Only a year before, a young assistant in the Paris Prefecture of Police, Alphonse Bertillon, had laid the cornerstone of modern criminology with his development of the 'bertillonage' system of measurements for criminals. And a year before that, in the pages of a magazine called Nature, a Scottish physician named Henry Faulds, made a number of observations about the 'skin-furrows in human fingers (which) ... may lead to the scientific identification of criminals.'

But in Victorian England it was not until 1871 that Parliament finally passed a bill providing for the registration of habitual criminals, complete with photographs and personal dossiers, whilst the system of finger printing did not gain official recognition until as late as 1895.

Sherlock Holmes represented a revolutionary trend, therefore, in the investigation of crime. The public of the time certainly shared his contempt for the official detective force but they were also understandably puzzled by his approach. This was really because Holmes was first and foremost a pioneer of new techniques which very soon would change the face of Scotland Yard.

The detective's own wide knowledge of classic murder cases and of the circumstances of their victims' demise certainly assisted him in the detection of crime and the speed with which he reached his conclusions. Later in that same account by Dr. Watson, Holmes mentions that "The forcible administration of poison is by no means a new thing in criminal annals. The cases of Dolsky in Odessa, and of Leturier in Montpellier, will occur at once to any toxicologist." One suspects that the Commonplace and other books which cluttered the interior of 221B Baker Street, far from gathering dust, were stuffed to the brim with excerpts from The Police Gazette and cuttings from the newspaper reports of sensational murder trials of the period. And Holmes' brain was, we recall, like an attic, from which all types of useful data could be extracted in order to provide a useful comparison.

Any criminologist knows that the existence of a pattern in the crime of murder is of supreme importance to the investigator. And the recognition of a pattern in the early stages of an investigation gave Holmes an advantage over the official police force of the day, whose methods lacked a definite system. It is therefore not surprising that he was once compared to Alphonse Bertillon, the great French criminologist. Holmes recommended that the most practical thing a detective could do was to "shut yourself up for three months and read twelve hours a day at the annals of crime," and pointed out that "It's all been done before, and will be again." For that reason, he spent much of his professional career absorbing and becoming expert upon a wide range of specialised knowledge, including tobacco ashes, cryptography, newspaper types, perfumes, toxicology, the dating of documents, the typewriter and its relation to crime, bicycle tyres, tattoos, footsteps, the influence of the trade on the form of the hand, and the names and trademarks of the world's major gunmaking firms. He also showed considerable interest in anatomy, an interest which Watson described as "accurate but unsystematic," and twice applied this knowledge in the form of practical experiments. Although he claimed to have investigated over five hundred cases in the course of his career, a surprisingly small number (38%) dealt with murder. Fourteen of these resulted in the murderers being arrested or killed, three involved non-human agents, and in all fourteen Holmes made a successful analysis. In five other cases, Holmes succeeded in identifying the criminal but the murderers escaped the reach of the law, and in four other cases Holmes gave the murderers their liberty, because there were extenuating circumstances involved. Today's forensic scientist would have found the range of murder cases fascinating. Among the causes of death were gassing, poisoning, asphyxiation, and death from head injuries, comprising a variety of blunt instruments and guns. In the vast majority of these cases, a quick eye for detail at the scene of the crime led Holmes to the murderer with remarkable rapidity. The principles he espoused in the detection of crime are no different today than they were in 1880: the power of observation, the power of deduction, and a wide range of exact knowledge. In a period when forensic science was still in its infancy, Holmes was a man at the top of his league, and this accounts for much of his success as an investigator. He made full use of many of the forensic fields now permanently established: toxicology, ballistics, document examination, even graphology. One of the most useful areas of forensic investigation is that of contact traces, which encompasses the principle that an encounter between victim and murderer leads often to small traces of contact, e.g. blood, fibres, hair. One recalls that one section of the rooms at 221B was devoted to the chemical retort and the microscope especially for this purpose. These days, of course, no one man or woman investigates the causes and effects of a murder. The whole thing is a complex process, involving a variety of experts. In Holmes' day, there was no alternative but to become Jack of All Trades. He was sometimes called upon to be police surgeon, forensic analyst, and detective, all at one time. That he did this with such a measure of success places him in a unique position in the annals of crime. In the field of fictional Victorian criminal investigation, he remains unique.

## A  FORENSIC A – Z TO THE HOLMES STORIES

ACETONES (Ger. keton)

The simplest of those organic compounds consisting of a carbonyl group united to two like or unlike alkyl radicals. In COPP, Holmes did some research into their properties. Possibly he may have been interested in ketosis, an excessive formation in the body of acetone bodies, due to incomplete oxidation of fats - a condition which occurs in diabetes.

ACID

The generic name applied to several chemical compounds. Acids are mentioned several times in Sherlock Holmes stories. We learn of Holmes leaving acid stains in the rooms at Baker Street, Holmes' chemical table was acid stained and his hands were often discoloured with acids (STUD). However, on only one occasion

are we told of his use of acids in a case. This happens in NAVA where an acid test is being used to determine a man's guilt. Unfortunately for the reader, the name of the potential criminal is not given: "You come at a crisis, Watson. If this paper remains blue, all is well. If it turns red, it means a man's life." When the litmus paper does turn red, Holmes sends several telegrams to the authorities. We are told nothing else about this case or indeed the chemistry used to determine guilt. Elsewhere, the smell of hydrochloric acid informed Watson that Holmes had been involved in chemical work (IDEN) and carbolic acid is mentioned twice. Watson uses carbolic acid to dress the mutilated thumb of the unfortunate Victor Hatherley (ENGR) and in CARD, Holmes realises that carbolic acid was not used in order to preserve to severed ears, indicating that they were not sent to Sarah Cushing by a medical student. Sulphuric acid is also mentioned in two of the  stories, BLUE and ILLU. In both cases the substance is described as vitriol. In the former case, we understand that a vitriol throwing incident forms part of the history of the blue carbuncle, whilst in the latter, Kitty Winter, who has reason enough to hate the predatory Baron Von Gruner, throws sulphuric acid into his face. The horrific effects of a vitriol throwing are vividly described in that story: '...the butler and several footmen ran in from the hall. I remember that one of them fainted as I knelt by the injured man and turned that awful face to the light of the lamp. The vitriol was eating into it everywhere and dripping from the ears and the chin. One eye was already white and glazed . The other was red and inflamed. The features which I had admired a few minutes before were now like some beautiful painting over which the artist has passed a wet and foul sponge. They were blurred, discoloured, inhuman, terrible.'
Whilst vitriol throwing is comparatively rare in Britain, it is still a

popular means of exacting revenge in countries in the Middle East.

## AGONY COLUMNS

As an aid to his criminal investigations, Holmes found that the agony columns of the daily newspapers were invaluable. Agony columns had existed in Victorian society since the 1860s, both in the popular newspapers of the period and in ladies magazines. Holmes was an avid reader of the newspapers where he garnered much of his knowledge about the most sensational crimes of his times. In NOBL, he told Watson that he read both the criminal news and the agony columns and also mentioned that he kept a book in which he filed news cuttings. Elsewhere, this is referred to as the 'commonplace book' and appears to have run into several volumes, including an index which he refers to as 'good old index'. Watson also mentions the scrapbooks at Baker Street (EMPT), and in REDC reference is made to the filing of the contents of the agony columns on a daily basis. In VALL, he refers to the cryptic messages contained in the agony columns and in REDC he talks about the 'unmitigated bleat' of their messages:"What a chorus of crones, cries and bleatings! What a ragbag of singular happenings! But surely the most valuable hunting ground that ever was given to a student of the unusual." Holmes frequently advertised in the papers in order to expedite a case. Advertisements were tried as part of the search for Lady Frances Carfax (LADY), and he also advertised in the evening newspapers in order to find Henry Baker (BLUE) and to discover Joseph Harrison's cab driver (NAVA). Mycroft Holmes also used this facility in order to advertise for Paul and Sophy Kratides in The Greek Interpreter, advertising in the London dailies.

AIR GUN

Airguns feature prominently in two of the Holmes stories but most attention to an airgun is given in EMPT where Holmes is targeted by his opponent, Colonel Sebastian Moran. Holmes describes Moran's weapon as 'admirable and unique... Noiseless and of tremendous power.' Invented in the 16th century, airguns were pneumatic pump powered weapons which could be fired several times a minute and which had the advantage of being noiseless. The guns operate on the basis of compressed air by means of a plunger fitted to the bore. In some forms of airgun compressed spring is activated by means of the trigger and this in turn forces there to project the ball. The air gun used in the attempted murder of Holmes was we learn, invented by Von Herder. It was later given to the Scotland Yard Museum. Another airgun, made for Count Sylvius by Straubenzee, was never actually used in order to shoot Holmes. (MAZA).

ALIENIST

In CREE, Watson expressed the opinion that Professor Presbury's behaviour should require an alienist, one who treats mental illness. In SIXN, he talked about the modern French psychologists' idea of monomania and Inspector Lestrade believed that whoever was destroying the Napoleonic busts was s monomaniac. In ENGR Victor Hatherley wondered if the girl Elsie might be a monomaniac. In the 19th century, monomania was regarded as a form of partial insanity, conceived as a single pathological preoccupation. The term was coined by the French psychiatrist Jean Esquirol in 1810. He and his fellow alienists defined three categories of the disease, intellectual, emotional and volitional. He believed that emotional monomania was that in which the patient was obsessed with one emotion or idea, the idee fixe. The concept of monomania was popular among 19th-century writers. Edgar Allan Poe was preoccupied with the notion of monomania and used this as the basis for several of his stories, including The Black Cat (about a man who fears his cat and then kills it, adopts another cat, then kills his wife), The Oval Portrait (about a painter who is obsessed with painting his wife,) and The Tell-tale Heart (about a man who is obsessed with an old man's vulture- like eye). The idea of monomania also crops up in Herman Melville's Moby Dick where the central character, Capt Ahab is obsessed with the notion of killing the white whale: 'But, as in his narrow flowing monomania, not one jot of a hence broad madness had been left behind, so in that broad madness, not one jot of his great natural intellect had perished... So that far from having lost his strength, Ahab, to that one end, did now possess thousandfold more potency than ever he had sanely brought to bear upon any reasonable object.'

## ALKALOID

A word applied to compounds such as quinine, morphine, caffeine. In STUD Stamford tells Watson that he could imagine Holmes giving a friend a 'pinch of the latest vegetable alkaloid – not out of malevolence, you understand, but simply out of a spirit of enquiry.' In studying the alkaloidal poisons, Holmes chose to investigate the oldest group of drugs known to man. However, since the last century the crude vegetable drugs like strychnine, to which this variety belongs, have declined (except for digitalis which is still used for the treatment of heart conditions) and the synthetic drugs have come to the fore.
The word "alkaloid" refers to the active ingredient of a drug or poison. They are basic substances that can combine with acids to form salts ( e.g. morphine tartrate, atropine sulphate).

# The Criminological Sherlock Holmes

In his letter to Sherlock Holmes (STUD), Tobias Gregson, the Scotland Yard detective, writes that one of his officers has discovered the body of a well dressed gentleman, bearing a card in his pocket with the name "Enoch J. Drebber" printed thereon. He goes on to point out that "There had been no robbery, nor is there any evidence as to how the man met his death." However, a visit by Holmes and Watson to No. 3 Lauriston Gardens, reveal the inadequacy of the detective's observations. Watson has often been noted for his inaccuracy, but the description he provides of the deceased has a clinical ring to it which does justice to his medical training:

"(The body)... was that of a man about forty-three or forty-four years of age, middle-sized, broad-shouldered, with crisp curling black hair, and a short, stubby beard... His hands were clenched and his arms thrown abroad, while his lower limbs were interlocked, as though his death struggle had been a grievous one. On his rigid face there stood an expression of horror, and, as it seemed to me, of hatred, such as I have never seen upon human features. This malignant and terrible contortion, combined with the low forehead, blunt nose, and prognathous jaw, gave the dead man a singularly sinuous and ape-like appearance, which was increased by his writhing, unnatural posture..."

Watson is describing the classic symptoms of rictus sardonicus, which are a feature of alkaloid poisoning and tetanus. Naturally, he does not reveal the cause of Drebber's death to the reader, since he has reasons to keep him in suspense. All he allows himself is to quote Holmes' own comment to Lestrade and Gregson: "Poison," before the detective strides off, leaving them open-mouthed behind him.
Later, Holmes allows himself a little more latitude when he explains to Watson:

"Having sniffed the dead man's lips, I detected a slightly sour smell, and I came to the conclusion that he had poison forced upon him from the hatred and fear expressed upon his face.... Do not imagine that it was a very unheard-of idea. The forcible administration of poison is by no means a new thing in criminal annals. The cases of Dolsky in Odessa, and of Leturier in Montpellier, will occur at once to any toxicologist."

Nowhere in the narrative does Holmes state that the poison is a specific alkaloid, but then he is not required to do so. However, there are a number of indications that the substance used by Jefferson Hope on his unfortunate victim was our old friend strychnine.
The experiment carried out on the ailing terrier at 221B Baker Street does much to justify our choice of one of the very powerful alkaloids.

"With a perfect shriek of delight he rushed to the box, cut the other pill in two, dissolved it, added milk, and presented it to the terrier. The unfortunate creature's tongue seemed hardly to have been moistened in it before it gave a convulsive shiver in every limb, and lay as rigid and lifeless as if it had been struck by lightning."

The convulsive symptoms shown both by Drebber and the terrier suggest a poison which affects the spinal cord and produces the tetanic spasms. There a number of contenders for this: strychnine seems most likely, since we have it on good authority that the terrier was affected immediately, and strychnine is a fast-acting alkaloid. A large dose will kill a small mammal instantly. To Holmes the investigator, the difference between tetanus and strychnine poisoning would have been obvious at a glance, for with tetanus, the symptoms manifest themselves over a period of days, and with tetanus, opisthotonos does not occur until some days after the condition has been established. Death from strychnine may be quick and its effect sudden.

## AMALGAM

(L. L. amalgama) A combination of mercury and solid metal. Holmes assumed that the coiners at Eyford (ENG) had used an amalgam to take the place of silver, but since nickel and tin were discovered in the outhouse this seems unlikely.

## ANALYSIS

SEE Deduction

ANARCHISM   (Gr. anarchia: leaderlessness) The teaching of the anarchists; that group of 19th century idealists whose ideal of society was one without government of any kind; also, one who seeks to advance such a system by acts of terrorism. The anarchist sect emerged circa 1872 and suffered considerably from a reactionary press in Europe. Much of the romanticism attached to their movement can be attributed to the popular writers of the later 19th century (Chesterton, Conrad, etc.). Morse Hudson commented (typically) that nobody but an anarchist would go around smashing busts of Napoleon.
(SIXN)

## ANATOMY

In STUD, at the time of their first meeting, Watson described Holmes' knowledge of anatomy has accurate but unsystematic, and years later in FIVE alluded to this earlier description. Also in STUD, Holmes caused some interest by his beating of cadavers in the dissecting rooms at St Bartholomew's Hospital, an exercise which was to determine how far bruises can be produced after death. No doubt Holmes would have been familiar with the pioneering work of the British pathologist Alfred Swaine Taylor who had trained in Paris and taught forensic medicine in London. He was the author of an influential work on pathology and toxicology. Holmes' detailed examination of the corpse in STUD, where 'his nimble fingers were flying here, there, and everywhere, feeling, pressing, unbuttoning, examining,' is a reminder of Taylor's instruction in his 1873 work, A Manual of Medical Jurisprudence:

'The first duty of the medical jurist is to cultivate a faculty of minute observation... A medical man, when he sees a dead body, should notice everything. He should observe everything which could throw a light on the production of wounds or other injuries found upon it. It should not be left to a policeman to say whether there were any marks of blood on the dress or on the hands of the deceased, or on the furniture of the room. The dress of the deceased as well as body should always be closely examined on the spot by the medical man.'

There were few forensic experts on hand at scenes of crime in Holmes' day, so it is hardly surprising that he acted in the way that he did. His knowledge of dissection is demonstrated in CARD where he dismisses the idea that the severed ears sent to an old lady are from a dissecting room, making the point that the ears have been packed in salt, a procedure which will not indicate the actions of a medical student. The topic of anatomy also crops up in CREE where we discover that Professor Morphy held the chair of Comparative Anatomy at Camford University, and in HOUN where Dr Mortimer and Charles Baskerville 'spent many a charming evening' discussing 'the comparative anatomy of the Bushman and the Hottentot.'

## ANEURISM, AORTIC

(Otherwise: aneurysm: Gr. aneurysm) A condition of the heart in which the aorta (the great trunk of the arterial system) swells out. Often caused by syphilis. Jefferson Hope (STUD) died as a result of this condition.

## APOPLEXY

Apoplexy is a term meaning a stroke of bodily disablement connected with some diseased condition of the brain. In persons subject to heart disease, a clot may form in the valve of the heart and be carried to the brain. The occurrence of this embolism produces the sudden effects witnessed in apoplexy. The person who suffers such an attack becomes suddenly deprived of consciousness and lies in a deep sleep, exhibiting a flushed face and slow pulse. Death may occur within a few hours. Apoplexy is referred to on two occasions in the Holmes saga. In CREE, Colonel Barclay suffered an apoplectic attack and fell, hitting his head on the fender. Traces of blood and hair were noted there by Holmes. He was found dead in the morning-room of Lachine, Aldershot, between 9 and 10 P.M. on Monday, September 9. The maid heard an altercation between Col. Barclay and his wife. She received no reply when knocking and found the door locked from the inside. Hearing screams, the coachman, whom the maid had summoned to her assistance, ran round to the outside of the house and gained entry via the French windows. He discovered Mrs. Barclay, stretched unconscious on a couch and the Colonel lying with his head on the ground near the corner of the fender. A ragged cut was discovered, some two inches long, at the back of his head, caused apparently by a violent blow from a blunt weapon. This surmise was later discovered to be incorrect. Close to the body was a club of hard carved wood with a bone handle. This was later discovered to belong to Henry Wood, Mrs. Barclay's visitor. In GLOR, James Armitage suffered an attack of apoplexy after receiving a letter posted in Fordingham. The letter warned him that Hudson (the sailor who had been blackmailing him) had "told all," thereby revealing Armitage's part in the Gloria Scott mutiny years earlier. Armitage's mouth and eyelids "were all puckered on one side," a condition which spread, causing paralysis and eventual coma.

## AQUA TOFANA

In the Daily Telegraph (as quoted in STUD) Aqua Tofana is alluded to. In the 17th century in Italy a woman called Teofania di Adamo went about the streets of Rome and Naples selling a liquid which was described as the Manna of St Nicholas of Bari. This was described as a cosmetic. A small amount of the substance caused death. The poison became quickly known as Aqua Tofana. In both cities, husbands started to suffer from digestive problems which ultimately led to death. When eventually Teofania was confronted with these deaths by the authorities, she entered a convent but was eventually expelled. When questioned, this Italian poisoner confessed to more than 600 murders and was strangled, following a lengthy investigation. It is believed that her daughter carried on the family tradition.

## ARAB, STREET

Homeless or slum boy, a child of the street. The Baker Street
Irregulars, Holmes' band of street urchins, were referred to as
'street arabs'. The O.E.D. has the original as 'Arab of the City' or
'City Arab', and quotes (1848) Guthrie, Plea for the Ragged
School: 'The Arab of the City.' A speech made in Parliament by
Lord Shaftsbury 16 June 1848 refers to 'City Arabs.. .are like
tribes of lawless freebooters, bound by no obligations, and utterly
ignorant or utterly regardless of social duties'.

## ARSON

The burning of a dwelling house with malicious intent. In
NORW, John Hector Macfarlane was suspected of arson and
Moriarty's men set fire to Holmes' rooms in Baker Street (FINA).

## ASSAULT

The attempt to inflict injury on someone. In the Holmes stories,
assaults on individuals occur no less than 18 times. See NAVA,
REIG, ENGR, SOLI, HOUN, 3GAB, NORW, SPEC, VEIL,
BLAC, GLOR, BLUE, IDEN, MAZA, STUD, ILLU.

## ATAVISM

The theory of ancestral characteristics which recur in the human
being, or in pathology, the recurrence of the disease from an

ancestor. In GREE Holmes discusses the question of atavism. In EMPT he went further to explain that the individual represents in his development the procession of his ancestors and then to turn for good or evil stands for a strong influence on the line of his pedigree, the person becoming the epitome of the history of his family, this being evident in the character of Col Sebastian Moran. He also believed that Professor Moriarty had hereditary tendencies of a diabolical nature and that there was in the Prof's blood a criminal strain which was heightened by his extraordinary mental powers (FINA). Holmes explained his own capabilities in terms of this theory and on two other occasions, HOUN and SPEC, used the theory to explain the actions of criminals. It is clearly evident that Holmes was influenced by the theories of the early criminologist, Cesare Lombroso, who believed that criminals were essentially throwbacks to Neanderthal man. Lombroso was influential in Latin America and subsequently achieved wider fame.

Lombroso shared more than just the distinction of being a contemporary to Holmes. He was one of those great thinkers of the nineteenth century who had the foresight to apply inductive methods of modern science to the study of the human animal. While he was not the first to search for the causes of human behaviour in the physiological and mental features of the individual (Galenus, Gall and Morel had preceded him in this), he was indeed alone in the extent to which he carried this type of analysis. Like Holmes, his teachings aroused much opposition, but they were based firmly on an exact scientific method.

It was in fact L'Uomo Delinquente which set forth Lombroso's main theory: that crime is almost entirely conditioned by the anthropological characteristics of the criminal. It was in the years to follow that the objections to this work snowballed. Some critics objected to it on moral grounds: others refuted it as unprovable.

Lombroso's picture of the criminal was of a type who clearly reproduced the characteristics of an earlier phase in humanity. And he found his parallels in both the plant and animal worlds. He pointed out that the lower species and primitive races share many habits which in themselves cannot be regarded as criminal but when applied to civilized man they then afford this term. For example, homicide is frequently practised and sanctioned, as is infanticide and sometimes cannibalism among certain aboriginal races.

Children were also attractive to Lombroso's field of study, simply because in its first year or more of life a child lacks any moral standard and its development is affected totally by its environment. Therefore there are many abnormal children in whom a criminal tendency manifests itself.

Lombroso's comparison with the skulls of the insane showed him that criminals surpassed the insane in most of the cranial anomalies. But when he came to compare savage and prehistoric skulls the atavistic nature of these anomalies became clear to him. And he added: "Note that these cranial alterations bear only upon the most visible modifications of the intellectual centre, the alterations of volume and form."

That Holmes was profoundly influenced by Lombroso's controversial conclusions seems obvious. At that time Lombroso was (apart from Bertillon) virtually alone in the field of criminological theory and it was not until the turn of the century that forensic medicine and all the innovations of scientific study began to enrich the subject. Holmes would therefore have looked deeply into Lombroso's study, although with a critical eye. Holmes' monograph on tattooing is a point of immediate reference between these two pioneers. (See TATTOOING.) It is only a pity that we do not possess a copy of the Holmes contribution. But the importance of tattooing becomes apparent in a number of Watson's reported cases. The classic example is that of Jabez Wilson who had a fish tattooed above his right wrist in a shade of pink which Holmes noticed was "quite peculiar to

China." (REDH) However, in a much earlier case, (GLOR)
Trevor Senior had the initials "J.A." tattooed on his elbow. These
markings did not go unnoticed by the young criminologist.
The reason for Holmes' passionate interest in the subject of
tattooing becomes apparent when we examine the claims made
for it in Lombroso's "Homme Criminel" (Paris 1895).

'One of the most characteristic traits of primitive man or of the
savage is the facility with which he submits himself to this
operation, surgical rather than aesthetic, and of which the name
even has been furnished to us by an Oceanic idiom.... Tattooing is
in fact one of the essential characteristics of primitive man and of
the man who is still living in a savage state.'

It is interesting to see what Lombroso has to say about these
"savages". Holmes too was fascinated by the behaviour of
"primitive" peoples and their appearance is marked in more than
one of Dr. Watson's chronicles (WIST, SIGN). Perhaps the most
memorable of these people was Tonga, a native of the Andaman
islands. Holmes' gazetteer, it will be remembered, made some
very unfair comments about the Andamaners, referring to them as
"naturally hideous, having large, misshapen heads, small, fierce
eyes, and distorted features." They are also described as "fierce,
morose and intractable." Lombroso referred to the Andamaners in
a somewhat kinder vein. They had, he observes, "so restless a
disposition that they remain not more than two or three days in
the same place.... This attitude seems to be the result of a passage
between physiopsychic inertia and an intermittent need of violent
and unrestrained physical and moral excitation, which always
goes with inertia and impulsiveness."

The subject of children in the Canon has been dealt with before.
What are interesting, however, are those cases involving children
who display criminal and sometimes pathological tendencies.

# The Criminological Sherlock Holmes

Lombroso's fascination lay precisely in this field. He believed that not only was pathological behaviour absorbed by children from their progenitors but that it was genetically inevitable. A criminal was born with his potential criminality intact. Whether he overcame those tendencies natural to him was then a matter of free choice.

The mental characteristics Lombroso noted: excitability, moodiness, precocity, coupled with those physiological details already described are clearly delineated in The Adventure of the Copper Beeches. Mrs. Ruscastle's step-daughter provides a classic example:

'I have never met so utterly spoilt and so ill-natured a little creature. He is small for his age, with a head which is quite disproportionately large. His whole life appears to be spent in an alternation between savage fits of passion and gloomy intervals of sulking. Giving pain to any creature weaker than himself seems to be his own idea of amusement, and he shows quite remarkable talent in planning the capture of mice, little birds, and insects.'

Holmes' quick appreciation of the peculiar Ruscastle menage is evident to anyone reading the story, and lends substance to the theory that Holmes had a thorough understanding of Lombroso's observations about the affinity between child immorality and the behavioural traits of the criminal. However, this is not an isolated case. In The Sussex Vampire, for instance, the villain of the piece is the young boy, Jacky. In an act of jealousy Ferguson's son fires a poisoned arrow at his younger brother. The crime is quickly spotted by Holmes:

'It was at this moment (observes Watson) that I chanced to glance at Holmes, and saw most singular intentness in his expression. His face was as set as if it had been carved out of old ivory, and his eyes... had glanced for a moment at father and child....'

Holmes, who has watched the boy intently, observes in his face "such jealousy, such cruel hatred, as I have seldom seen in a human face."

In HOUN, the business of the family portraits at Baskerville Hall and Holmes' intuitive reckoning of Stapleton as a throwback to the wicked Hugo directly confirms Lombroso's theory of atavism. Holmes' acceptance of genetic duplication is total and unquestioning:

"Yes (he observes), it is an interesting instance of a throwback, which appears to both physical and spiritual. A study of family portraits is enough to convert a man to the doctrine of reincarnation."

I think the reader will understand why I have emphasized those key words. They demonstrate the extent to which Holmes had accepted the ideas of Lombroso by this stage in his career and begun to apply them to his own methods.

ATKINSON BROTHERS

"From time to time I heard some vague account of his doings:... of his clearing up of the singular tragedy of the Atkinson brothers at Trincomalee. . ." (SIGN)

The Atkinson tragedy and Holmes' involvement in this episode has been fully chronicled by Lt. Cdr. G.S. Stavert (SHJ. Vol 13 Nos. 1 & 2). Holmes, he speculates, had gone on a long sea voyage to Trincomalee, owing to the grave state of his health. Thomas Atkins, the "young son of Corporal Atkins" of the Argyll and Sutherland Highlanders, was found apparently strangled near the entrance to a Buddhist temple, a few miles outside the village at Trincomalee. On examining the boy's body, Holmes was able to deduce that the boy had fallen under the chariot of "Jagganath" during the festivities held by the Hindis and his neck was then broken by the wheel of the chariot. Colonel Forbes-Robertson of the Argyll and Sutherland Highlanders was eternally indebted to the detective for his clearing up of his mystery, especially since blame had been apportioned to the chief Buddhist monk on the island of Ceylon. Holmes' intervention thus prevented serious religious conflict between the Hindis and Buddhists.

## BARITSU-WRESTLING

Bartitsu, a system of self-defence named after E.W. Barton-Wright who introduced the system into England in 1899.Holmes claims to have been familiar with it in 1891 – an anachronism. He was probably referring to jujitsu, a method of fighting involving techniques of hitting, kicking, immobilizing holds, etc. which arose from the feudal warrior clans in 17th century Japan.   It was his knowledge of Bartitsu (misspelt by Watson) which enabled Holmes to defeat Professor Moriarty.

## BARYTA

(Gr. barys, heavy) Barium monoxide. Holmes claimed to have been analysing a sample of bisulphate of baryta, a substance which does not exist. (IDEN) More probably he was experimenting with baryta paper, a paper coated on one side with an emulsion of barium sulphate and gelatine. This substance is used for photographic printing paper.

## BAKER STREET IRREGULARS

One important advantage Holmes gained over his rivals was the inexpensive employment of the gang of street children introduced to us in STUD as 'the Baker Street Irregulars'. The beggar children, or 'street arabs' as Watson calls them, were to be found everywhere. The police could do little about these children, partly because they were a source of great amusement to the general middle class public but also because they were extremely agile and evasive. The only place open to many of them was the workhouse and most of those refused to take responsibility for them. So they lingered in the streets where they cavorted, made a mischief of themselves or were sexually abused by child offenders and foreign sailors. The Telegraph Boy Scandal in which many prominent homosexuals were involved, pointed to the unrestricted abuse of young children who were left to roam the streets of Victorian London. Often children would be used by professional beggars to oust a rival from a much sought after 'patch' and were variously employed in the execution of street crime.

Holmes was quick to perceive the potential in these street urchins'. Unworried by the demands of an elementary education, they were available at all hours and could be relied upon to offer their services under the most unlikely of conditions. The workhouse didn't want them, the reformatories rejected them, but Mr. Sherlock Holmes of Baker Street paid them by the hour. The Irregulars appear in several of the stories (namely CROO, SIGN, STUD, HOUN and LADY) and appeared to be an indispensable part of the detective's data gathering. Apart from finding the missing Aurora in SIGN, they appear to have achieved a great deal else for Holmes. Wiggins ('the scarecrow') was clearly the leader of the pack but that Holmes used others in an individual capacity is certain. Simpson and Cartwright were employed separately on two occasions. Holmes' wages of a shilling a day provided a handsome remuneration. But what did they do for the rest of their time? Were they used just on an ad hoc basis or had Holmes other uses for them?

In later years we do not hear so much about the Irregulars. Perhaps they were disbanded and absorbed into the system of elementary education. Or perhaps Holmes found fewer occasions when he could use them. With such men as Mercer (CREE), Shinwell Johnson (ILLU) and Langdale Pike (3GAB) at large, the Irregulars may have seemed dangerous bait for hardened criminals. But I have a hunch that at least one of them, Wiggins, was to provide a continued service to the detective in his later years. Most commentators give the date of MAZA in which we encounter Billy the pageboy as 1903. This being the case, and assuming that 'Billy' Wiggins was roughly eleven or twelve in SIGN (1887), it would make him all of 28, which is highly unlikely. But if the assumption of 1903 is incorrect and the case belongs to an earlier year, it would indeed be possible that Wiggins was the page boy. That he had been pageboy for some years is evident from Watson's remark to him: 'You don't change, either'.

From the very outset of his career in STUD, it is clear that Holmes was dogged by a sharp social conscience in what was an uncaring age. His remarks about the boarding schools (NAVA), often quoted, show his concern with the welfare of young people from the lower classes and may be evidence of an impoverished upbringing. The Irregulars' enlistment shows one aspect of this concern and he probably provided them with more charity and assistance than we are aware of.

Aided by the newly emerging forensic methods and his own ingenious street detective force, Holmes had all the advantages over his competitors in the field.

## B DIVISION

A section of the Metropolitan Police Force responsible for sections of Chelsea, Victoria, Knightsbridge and Westminster. Inspector Bradstreet of B Division gave evidence against John

Horner after the theft of the blue carbuncle.

BELLADONNA

(Atropa belladonna) Otherwise deadly nightshade. The plant's leaves and roots are used to produce atropine, but also assist in the manufacture of cosmetics; hence Holmes' use of the substance in DYIN. Belladonna is so-called because Italian women discovered that the pupils of their eyes became greatly expanded if a drop of the juice of this herb were applied.

BERTILLON

There is little doubt that Holmes' studies embraced the as yet embryonic theories of Alphonse Bertillon. Later in his career Holmes pays a rather sardonic compliment to his famous rival on the shores of France: (HOUN)

MORTIMER: To the man of precisely scientific mind the work of Monsieur Bertillon must always appeal strongly.
HOLMES: Then had you not better consult him?

Alphonse Bertillon was virtually unknown in 1881. He began his career as a junior clerk in the Paris Prefecture and was a self-made man, lacking a formal education in science. There is, in fact, a curious similarity between him and Sherlock Holmes who also, it will be recalled, ranked as an outsider and demonstrated an extremely unorthodox approach to learning.
 Like Bertillon, Holmes also believed that it was not data itself that mattered but one's organisation of it. The organisation of data was Bertillon's chief claim to fame: Bertillonage. Bertillon's anthropometric method was a system based on certain key parts of the human body. The idea was that since no two human beings were identical, one could build up a composite picture of a

criminal, incorporating data such as the colour of eyes, hair, shape of nose, ears, body markings, etc. The data was placed on a card together with a full face and profile (this system is used by Scotland Yard today). He also used an apparatus which could be graduated to measure each portion of the anatomy. A Vertical Scale was fixed to the wall, from which also protruded calipers to gauge the head. There was also a stand to measure the feet and adjustable instruments for measuring the ears.

It is quite probable that Holmes' indirect snub to the grand master of the anthropometric method derived from a basic mistrust of the system. The problem was that of the complexity of the data that had to be collated and stored. Bertillon's system, relying as it does on a variety of different measurements, is cumbersome and virtually unmanageable when applied to large numbers of people. Although in its first year Bertillon's department of Judicial Identity was responsible for unmasking 291 men acting out false identities, its collaters were open to a considerable margin of error, despite their diligence. "My measurements are surer than any fingerprint pattern," Bertillon claimed, but the case of the two William Wests in America proved him to be more fallible than he had in fact assumed. Despite his scepticism about fingerprinting, Bertillon became the first European in October 1902 to solve a murder using fingerprints. He died in 1913.


BISULPHATE OF BARYTA

Barium hydrogen sulphate, an obscure chemical compound. Holmes had been asked to identify this compound at the conclusion of the Mary Sutherland affair (IDEN). See also baryta.


BLACKMAIL

Money which is extorted from the person or persons under the threat of exposure for an alleged offence. Holmes himself considered blackmail an extremely despicable crime. He claimed that Moriarty was the head of the criminal chain which ended with the minor criminal such as the blackmailer (VALL) and he also called Charles Augustus Milverton the 'King of the blackmailers.' Blackmailing his mentioned in 14 cases in the saga, including REDC, VALL, 3GAB, LADY, YELL, SCAN, REIG, GLOR, BLAC, SECO, BOSC, CHAS .

BLOODSTAINS

Holmes regarded bloodstains as an important aspect of criminal investigation and was instrumental in carrying out his own investigations into the tests which were then known to forensic science. He believed that he had discovered a reagent which was precipitated by haemoglobin and nothing else, a method he believed would supersede the conventional Guaiacum test. (See GUAIACUM test and HAEMOGLOBIN.)
Bloodstains feature in a number of cases, including REDC, where bloody footprints are discovered, SECO, where a carpet is bloodstained, but the stain does not correspond to the stain on the floor beneath it, TWIS, where the room Neville St Clair was last seen in has drops of blood. Bloodstains were also found at the house of Hugo Oberstein, and at Deep Dene House, blood traces were discovered on the stick belonging to John Hector MacFarlane's stick and also on the wall in the shape of a bloody thumbprint. In STUD, blood traces were also found at the scene of Stangerson's murder. Stangerson's body was discovered at 8 A.M. by Inspector Lestrade of Scotland Yard in a room at Halliday's Private Hotel. The room on the second floor was locked, and, on being forced, Lestrade saw Stangerson's body lying in a nightdress, huddled beside an open window. Since the

body was already rigid, Lestrade deduced that the victim had died at around 6 A.M. The word RACHE, meaning vengeance, was written above the body, in letters of blood. Bloodstains were found in the washbasin of the room and on the bedsheets, indicating that the murderer, Jefferson Hope, had washed his hands and wiped the blade of his knife clean before leaving by the window. The cause of death was a deep knife stab in the left side of the victim, which penetrated the heart.

## BLUDGEON

A short stick, weighted at one end. (See also life preserver.) The word's origin is unknown and does not occur before the 18th century. In early 18th century usage it is spelt as 'Bailey, Bludgeon', and defined as an 'oaken stick or club'. Holmes was once attacked by a 'rough with a bludgeon'. Source: GREE; FINA.

## BOOK OF LIFE

See DEDUCTION

## BOXER CARTRIDGES

Centre-fire cartridges named after their inventor, Edward Mourner Boxer (1822-98). Holmes used a supply of 'a hundred Boxer cartridges' to help adorn a wall of the Baker Street sitting-room with 'a patriotic V.R. done in bullet-pocks'. Source: MUSG

## BRACELETS

(Victorian sl.) Handcuffs. Jonathan Small (SIGN) referred to the 'bracelets upon my wrists'. So also did Athelney Jones when speaking of John Clay. Cf. Scott's Harold Dauntless, iv, viii: 'His bracelets of iron - his bed in our towers.' By 1883 it was common usage (cf. Pall Mall Gazette, 1883). Source: SIGN, Ch.12; REDH

## BRINVILLERS

The Marquis of (1630 to 1676), a notorious French murderess who was said to have poisoned several members of her own family. See AQUA TOFANA.

## BRUISE

Holmes raised some controversy by his beating corpses in dissecting rooms at St Bartholomew's Hospital with a stick. He did this in order to verify how far bruises can be produced after death. (STUD).

## BUCK-SHOT (CARTRIDGES)

Cartridges filled with small pieces of lead, designed for the shooting of buck or deer. The weapon which killed Birdy Edwards was loaded with these. Source: VALL, Ch.4

## CAMBERWELL POISONING CASE (1887)

"The year' 87 furnished us with a long series of cases.... Among my headings ... I found an account of... the Camberwell poisoning case."

Was this a case of a woman poisoner, one wonders? Holmes' classic remark about the "most winning woman I ever knew was hanged for poisoning three little children," (SIGN) could be a direct reference to this case. Major Arthur Griffiths' Mysteries of Police and Crime (1898) contains an impressive list of female poisoners which only goes to back up Holmes' misogynist views.

## CANARY

In Victorian East End slang, the word canary refers to a female sentry posted in the street during a burglary in order to alert the intruders should a beat policeman approach. In BLAC, reference is made to the arrest of Wilson who was a notorious Canary Trainer. His arrest removed a plague spot from the East End of London.

## CARBINE

(Fr. carabine, from carabineer, a soldier of the 6th Dragoon Guards, armed with a short light rifle) Hence, a short rifle used in place of a side arm by artillery and cavalry. Source: SIGN; HOUN

## CARBOLIC or RECTIFIED SPIRITS

1.Carbolic acid (a disinfectant).
2.Purified alcohol spirit. Both substances were used to preserve medical specimens. Holmes refers to these substances when discussing the severed ears in CARD. See also ACID.

## CARBOLIZED BANDAGES

Bandages impregnated with carbolic acid, a strong antiseptic. Watson applied these to Victor Hatherley's wound (ENGR), a method which today would be frowned upon because of their effect upon the surface of the skin.

## CARBONARI

(It.: literally, charcoal burners) Members of a secret political association formed in the Kingdom of Naples in the early 19th Century, whose aim was to introduce a republican government. Alluded to in The Daily Telegraph article about the murder of Enoch Drebber. Source: STUD, Ch.6

CARDSHARPER

(Fr. carte, sharper, a cheat: Sl.) A cheat at cards. Moriarty stood at the head of a criminal chain which ended with 'the minor criminal such as the cardsharper'. Source: VALL

CAROTID ARTERY

(Gr. karotides, pl. - karos, sleep, the ancients supposing that deep sleep was caused by the compression of the artery(ies)). One of the two large arteries which carries blood to the head and brain. Young Willoughby Smith's carotid artery had been severed. Source: GOLD; CREE

CATALEPSY

(Gr. katalepsis, seizure) A state of more or less complete insensibility, with bodily rigidity. The presumed Russian patient who came to see Percy Trevelyan was supposed to be suffering from this condition. Catalepsy is a rare condition but was a popular subject among nineteenth century fiction-writers, particularly Poe. Source: RESI

CATARACT

(L. cataracta: Gr. kataraktes, portcullis) An opaque condition of the lens of the eye, unaccompanied by inflammation. Ronald

Adair's mother suffered from this condition. Cf. Bourde, Brev. Health (1547), lxvi, 28b: 'A Catharact, the which doth let a man to se perfytly.' Source: EMPT.

CATARACT KNIFE

(L. cataracta: Gr. kataraktes, portcullis) A small, delicate knife which is common in the removal of the lens of the eye in cataract surgery. A knife of this type was found among the personal effects of John Straker.. Source: SILV.

CHEMISTRY

Watson describes Holmes' knowledge of chemistry as profound (STUD), yet elsewhere as eccentric (FIVE), and mentions that the Baker Street rooms were always full of chemicals (MUSG). He often is described as carrying out experiments in his chemical corner and as a younger man at St Bartholomew's Hospital also conducted analysis. Holmes records that upon retirement he would devote himself to chemical research (FINA). After his visit to Norfolk he worked on experiments into organic chemistry (GLOR). See also ACETONES, CARBOLIC ACID, COAL TAR DERIVATIVES, CHLOROFORM, NITRITE OF AMYL PRUSSIC ACID and VITRIOL.

CHLOROFORM

(Gr. chloros, pale green) A limpid, mobile, colourless, volatile liquid (CHCL3) with a characteristic odour and a strong sweetish taste, used to induce insensibility. Lady Carfax was a victim of chloroform, as was Mrs Maberley. Source: 3GAB; LADY; LAST

CHOKEY

Gaol. (Victorian sl. Originally Anglo-Indian; from the Hindi hauki, shed, and adopted in England c.1850. From 1880 the word then meant 'imprisonment') Jonathan Small spoke of being 'stowed in chokey'. 'The Queen's Chokey was a prison diet of bread and water (1884). Source: SIGN, Ch.12.

## CIPHER

(O.Fr. cyfre: Ar. cifr: zero, empty) A secret form of writing. Holmes made it his business to know several forms of cipher and claimed to have authored a 'trifling monograph upon the subject, in which (he) analyse(d) one hundred and sixty separate ciphers'. Source: DANC; VALL, Ch.l.

## CIPHER TELEGRAM

A telegram in cipher. (See telegram and cipher) The cipher telegram was used by the Foreign office in SECO. Source: SECO.

## COAL-TAR DERIVATIVES

By-products of coal-tar, including ammonia, creosote, benzine, etc. obtained from the distillation of coal-tar. These were first identified in the mid nineteenth century. Holmes conducted research into their properties whilst at Montpellier. Source: EMPT

## COCAINE

(Sp. Quechua: coca) An alkaloid obtained from the leaves of the coca plant, a Peruvian shrub (erythroxylon coca) of a family akin to flax. Cocaine is a powerful narcotic and stimulant which in Holmes' day was a relative newcomer to the West. (Sigmund

Freud pioneered its use as an anaesthetic, although he later had misgivings about it.) Holmes was for many years a user of the drug with which he injected himself subcutaneously in a 7% solution. Source: FIVE; SCAN; SIGN; TWIS; YELL

## COINER

(L. cuneus, a wedge) Coining (or the manufacture of forged coins) was a large industry among the criminal fraternity of Victorian England. Colonel Lysander Stark was guilty of the offence of coining. Cf. Dickens, Nicholas Nickleby, Ch.X.: 'The longest-headed, queerest-tempered old coiner of gold and silver ever was.' Source: ENGR; SHOS.

## COMMONPLACE BOOK

A note or memorandum book (from commonplace, v.t., to make notes of; to put into a commonplace book). Holmes possessed a number of commonplace books which needed an index. In addition he maintained a number of scrapbooks and an index of biographies. He also appears to have filed the agony columns (q.v.) of the daily newspapers. The terms 'index', 'index of biographies' and 'commonplace book' often seem to be interchangeable. Source: BRUC; 3STU; FIVE; MUSG; REDC; ENGR; HOUN; SUSS; VEIL;IDEN; SCAN; PRIO; EMPT; MISS; SPEC; CREE.

## CONDYLE

(Gr. kondylos, knuckle) The protuberance at one end of a bone which forms a joint with another. Watson refers to the 'upper condyle of a human femur' - an impossibility since the femur has a condyle only at the lower (knee) end. Source: SHOS

## CONK-SINGLETON FORGEY CASE (1900)

"Watson.... get out the papers of the Conk-Singleton forgery case"
— SIXN

Forgery was an expanding industry in Victorian times. Among the more famous outrages were the Fletcher conspiracy (c. 1850) based on a system of forging wills in order to obtain unclaimed stock in public funds and the Burgess case, (1844) involving a consolidated annuity sum of £8,200.

## CONSUMPTION

(L. consumere, to destroy) Tuberculosis. Godfrey Staunton's wife died of this disease, as did Victor Trevor's sister. The O.E.D. has the word from 1398 onwards. Cf. Florence Nightingale's Nursing (1861), p. 26: 'That consumption is induced by the foul air of houses.. .is certain.' Source: MISS; GLOR

## COUNTERFEITING

Imitation money produced without the sanction of the state. In SHOS Holmes was able to trace the coiner by the zinc and copper filings in the seam of his cuff, while Dr Lysander Stark and his gang were coiners on a big scale. (ENGR). John Clay was also thought to have been a coiner. (REDH). See COINER.

## COVE

(Sl.) A man, a companion; fellow rogue. Partridge has this originating c.1560 and says that it is probably cognate with the Romany: cova, cova; 'that man'. Sam Merton, the prize-fighter, used the term. Source: MAZA.

## COVERT FOR PUTTING UP A BIRD

(Fr. couvrir) A covert is a bush used for cover by birds (such as pheasants). Holmes uses this sporting term to refer to his use of the agony columns (q.v.). Source: 3GAR.

## CRACKSMAN

(Sl., O.E. cracian, to crack) A burglar, especially a cracker of safes. Beddington (STOC) was a 'famous forger and cracksman' as was John Clay (REDH). Partridge has the originate as housebreaker (c.1810). The word is current in Lytton, Barham and Dickens. Source: STOC

## CRIB

(Sl. O.E. crib: Ger. krippe) A job. Jabez Wilson referred to 'a nice little crib all ready for me to step into' (REDH). (See also billet and berth). Athelney Jones referred to Jonathan Clay's capacity to 'crack a crib' (also in REDH), here referring to a burglary. Partridge has crib as 'to break open, burgle' from c.1720.   Cf. Dickens, Oliver Twist: 'There's one part we can crack, safe and softly.' Source: REDH; STOC

## CRYPTOGRAPHY

(see also CIPHER.) From the Greek meaning hidden secret and writing respectively. Practice and study of techniques for secure communication in the presence of third parties. In Holmes' day cryptography was synonymous with encryption, the conversion of information from readable state to apparent nonsense.

Decryption, which is also practised, is the reverse of encryption, moving from ciphertext back to plain text. Decryption in Holmes' era was dependent on the principle of frequency analysis.
Holmes' first encounter with Cipher occurs in GLOR which also was the first case he solved whilst he was a college student.
Victor Trevor, Holmes' college friend invites Holmes to spend his vacation at Trevor's father's estate in Norfolk. A man called Hudson, from Old Trevor's past arrives and blackmails him. After Hudson leaves, a note from from his friend Beddoes arrives: The text reads:

The supply of game for London is going steadily up. Head keeper Hudson, we believe, has been now told to receive all orders for flypaper and for preservation of your hen pheasant's life.

Holmes quickly solves the Cipher and works out that the code consists of instructions to read only every third word. This converts the code to the message: 'The game is up. Hudson has told all. Fly for your life.'

In the second code example in the Canon, (VALL), Holmes gets information from a contact in the Moriarty organisation from a man called Fred Porlock. This reads: 534 C2 13 127 36 31 4 17 21 41 Douglas 109 293 53 7 Birlstone 9 127 171.
Holmes works out that Porlock is using page 534 and column two of a book, but does not know which book is being used. He reasons that the book must be big enough to have 534 pages and two columns. Since the words Douglas and Birlstone don't appear on page 534 in the book, they are discarded. He deduces that the only book which would be likely to have such a format would be Whitaker's Almanac. The decoded message then is revealed: 'There is danger may come very soon one Douglas rich country now at Birlstone House Birlstone confidence is pressing.' The Cipher used in this instance is known as the Arnold Cypher.

Holmes' most famous use of cryptography occurs in DANC where a substitution cipher is solved using frequency analysis. In the first instance Holmes has only 15 characters of the first message from Chicago gangster, Abe Slaney. The message reads: Am here Abe Slaney. This leaves Holmes wishing for more data. After another five messages which total 62 characters he finally solves the Cipher, assigning the most frequent of the characters to E, a usual occurrence in the analysis of ciphers of this type. In all there are 17 e's in the 62 letters among the five messages. Holmes also deduces that the figure of a man holding a flag is the last letter in a word. Crucially he guesses that Elsie's name might be included in the message and this in turn leads him to the breakdown of the entire sequence of messages. The last message reads: 'Elsie, prepare to meet thy God.' Holmes travels to the Cubitt home in East Anglia but he is too late to prevent the death of Elsie's husband. He then uses the dancing men cipher in order to lure Abe Slaney to the house. In the same story he informs Watson that he has written a monograph in which he analyses 160 different forms of Cipher. It has frequently been pointed out that the cipher used in The Dancing Men is similar to that used by Edgar Allan Poe in his story, The Gold Bug.

## CURARE

"When I saw that little empty quiver beside the small bird-bow, it was just what I expected to see."
   – Sherlock Holmes, SUSS.

Curare is a South American arrow poison derived from the juice of a tree and which features in SUSS.
It was a dull, foggy November evening when Holmes and Watson reached the little village of Lamberhurst, Kent, 1 and the Tudor residence of Bob Ferguson, 2, the Mincing Lane tea broker. (SUSS.) Ferguson, who had been slightly acquainted with Dr

# The Criminological Sherlock Holmes

Watson, 3 some years ago, had returned to England with a Peruvian wife, a crippled son and a young baby. The attention bestowed on the youngest member of the Ferguson family provided the handicapped son, Jacky, with a motive for vengeance. Ferguson had brought with him a number of mementoes from his South American travels:

"The room (recalls Watson)... was a most singular mixture of dates and of places. The half-panelled walls ... were ornamented.., on the lower part by a line of well-chosen modern water-colours; while above, where yellow plaster took the place of oak, there was hung a fine collection of South American utensils and weapons, which had been brought, no doubt, by the Peruvian lady upstairs..."

Soon after their arrival at Cheeseman's, Holmes observes the family's pet spaniel (Carlo) which suffers a paralysis of the hind-legs. He at once realises that the dog has been used as an experimental vehicle for the "South American arrow poison" administered by arrows fired from a small bird-bow by the envious Jacky.

"I watched him as you fondled the child just now. His face was clearly reflected in the glass of the window where the shutter formed a background. I saw such jealousy, such cruel hatred, as I have seldom seen in a human face."

He concludes:

"If the child were pricked with one of those arrows dipped in curare or some other devilish drug, it would mean death if the venom were not sucked out."

Bearing in mind Holmes has not actually concluded that the

poison was curare, let us now examine the possibilities against it being such. W.S. Baring- Gould observes that: "Curare works by paralysing the thorax and chest muscles, not the legs, and it kills within minutes or not at all." 1

He goes on to quote from Mrs Eleanor S. Cole's article ("Holmes, Watson and the K'9's) 2, where she states that "the demonic little Jackie, filled with unusual remorse, sucked some of the poison from the dog's wound, yet not enough to leave him completely unimpaired."
Again, quoting F.A. Allen, 3, ("Devilish Drugs"): "The persistence of the paralytic effect... must be taken as traumatic or infective. This was strangely localized in the hind quarters of (the) dog ... a clumsy job in the back, near the cord, with a dirty half-soaped arrow-tip."
Finally, Baring-Gould quotes Dr George B. Roelle when he observes ("The Poisons Of The Canons" 4):

"... the effects of a non-fatal dose of (Curare) should wear off in a day. Consequently, the protracted lameness which the dog Carlo developed was probably due to spinal meningitis... or to mechanical injury or secondary infection of the sciatic nerve, as a result of the arrow puncture."

All of these statements about the effects of the poison curare are within the bounds of possibility except for that of Baring-Gould, who over-simplifies his case. In fact, paralysis commences in the hind extremities in warm blooded creatures, causing a numbness in the voluntary muscles. Eventually the animal ceases to move, the heart alone functioning. In the final stage death is caused by a cessation of the muscles in the chest area, respiration thus becoming impossible. During this latter period the muscles are subject to convulsive action and lacrymation and salivation also occur. It has been recorded that .00035 gramme of curarine per kilo of body weight will kill a small mammal in 10 to 15 minutes. And that of course is the problem we are confronted with, for the dog should not have survived at all after its ordeal. It is just possible that the young Jacky jabbed the dog lightly with the poisoned arrow tip to judge the effectiveness of the curare. In that case only a very small fraction of the dose would have entered the animal's bloodstream.

The other possibility (and this cast doubt on Holmes' credibility as an expert) is that the dog may have been suffering from a severe back injury or spinal meningitis. 5 If that were the case then the condition of the dog would have provided only the suggestion of foul play to Holmes. It was a case of inspired guesswork. (But as Holmes pointed out: " I never guess.")

If we are prepared to admit Holmes made a mistake about the dog, then the problem disappears. But what if the poison were not curare ?

Curare is obtained from the Wowali root and is one of several South American arrow poisons. Ineffective when taken orally, it is rapidly absorbed from the point of injection and reaches its peak of effectiveness about five minutes after the skin is punctured.

The active principle of curare is curarine (C10 11 15 N ), a crystallisable alkaloid which is soluble both in water and alcohol. When added to sulphuric acid it gives a pale violet colour which eventually turns to red. It has a brittle, brownish look under the microscope and possesses a shiny exterior. The poison affects first the motor nerves, then the blood vessels and finally the valves of the heart.

Well before 1600, curare was known among native people from the Atlantic to the Andes. But the secret of its ingredient, curarin, was not discovered for well over two hundred years. 6 The problem of identification was that different South American tribes created different combinations of the poison. There were three types of weapon used by them. The first was a

blowpipe arrow, about 15 inches long, smeared with the poison.
The second was an arrow shot from a small bow. These arrows
had a detachable tip which hung in the animal's flesh - a most
effective weapon. The third type of weapon was a spear made
from hard wood used to fell large mammals. It is the second
variety which formed part of the collection at Cheeseman's.
It soon became clear to Bernard that the type of curare being used
by natives in Guiana and Venezuela was different from the variety
found in Peru and Brazil.
He isolated two types of poison. One was Strychnos, 7, a
substance obtained from the outer bark of a tree. The other
variety was got from a woody vine. There are several varieties of
this vine to be found in South America, but all belong to the
genus known as Chondodendron. Whatever the source, however,
the process was the same for all tribes. The curare was boiled
down into a resinous mess and quite often other plants were
added, depending on the particular superstitions shared by the
witch doctor and his followers.
From 1939 onwards, pure supplies of curare became available to
pharmacologists in the West and the substance was purified. It
was found that small amounts of the poison were useful in
relaxing the abdominal muscles of patients undergoing
operations. Now of course it has been replaced by synthetic drugs
which are more predicable in their effects. 6
It is quite possible that the arrow tip used to spear both the
spaniel and the baby at the Cheeseman household was smeared
with a cocktail of substances, one part of which was curare. If the
cocktail were fairly dilute, the effects would not have been so
severe. At any rate, Mrs Ferguson's action was commendable,
considering the known potency of the poison.
As Holmes observes to Ferguson:

"Did it not occur to you that a bleeding wound may be sucked for
some other purpose than to draw blood from it ? Was there not a

Queen in English history who sucked such a wound to draw poison from it ?"9

It is a pity that Watson did not see fit to expound on the precise identity of the poison. Often in his recorded cases of The Master the relevant toxicological details are left unrecorded. To the man who cried: "Give me data", this must have been a serious omission.

One final point. It is assumed by Holmes and Watson that Mrs Ferguson has retired to her room because of her distress at discovering young Jacky's evil designs on her baby. But a reading of Watson's description of her condition would seem to suggest that possibly she too had been a victim of the poisonous weapons on display downstairs above the fireplace:

"On the bed a woman was lying who was clearly in a high fever. She was only half conscious... I stepped up to her with a few reassuring words, and she lay still while I took her pulse and temperature. Both were high, and yet my impression was that the condition was rather of mental and nervous excitement than of any actual seizure. "10

A woman of such strong and principled nature as Mrs Ferguson would hardly have given way to "brain fever". Far more likely that the stepson, having failed to eliminate the unwelcome baby who had claimed his mother's attentions, would now screw up his courage and wreak vengeance on the author of his frustrations. The story of Mrs Ferguson and her errant stepson is a remarkable one, not only for its toxicological interest, but also because it is a wonderful illustration of the tensions of family life. The curare is but the outward embodiment of those pent-up frustrations endured by Ferguson's alienated and crippled son.

Footnotes

1. Watson changes the name to Lamberley, yet the true identity of Bob Ferguson's house has been clearly demonstrated. See my own article in "Wheelwrightings," Vol 7, No 1, May 1984, pp. 24 - 26.
2. Known as "Cheeseman's. It was in fact the Owl House.
3. He had played against him as a three quarter rugby player for Richmond. Watson, it will be recalled, played for Blackheath Rugby Club.
1. "The Annotated Sherlock Holmes", Vol 2, p. 473, Note 17.
2. BSJ, Vol 1, No 1, New Series, Jan 1951, pp 25 - 9.
3. F.A. Allen, SHJ, Vol 3, No 3. Autumn 1957, pp. 12 - 14.
4. From "Leaves Of The Copper Beeches", pp. 91 - 6.
5. See Note 4.
6. It was the French physiologist, Claude Bernard, who discovered the mechanism of the alkaloid. By a series of experiments on frogs, he revealed that curare blocked impulses from the brain, thus causing loss of muscular control, and finally, respiratory asphyxiation. Bernard was awarded the Grand Prize of Physiology by the Academie des Sciences for his work.
7. Not to be confused with strychnine, which is derived from a relative of the plant found in South American countries. Its action is distinctly different.
8. See Norman Taylor's fascinating account of the history of this drug, "Plant Drugs That Changed The World", pp. 192 - 5. In fact, attempts to use curare in anaesthesia had been made as long ago as 1911 by Larwan. (For some years prior to this attempts had been made to use it as a treatment for lockjaw.) The fear of curare and its dangers prevented doctors from using it widely and it was not until 1943, when Griffith introduced curare into general anaesthetic practice, that the scientific world realised its therapeutic value.
9. The Queen was Eleanor of Castile, the wife of King Edward 1, who accompanied her husband to the Crusades and who is

supposed to have saved him from certain death by sucking a poisoned wound which he sustained in battle.
10.But it was a mere impression. He could not be sure.

## CUVIER, GEORGES

Cuvier, Georges Leopold, Baron, 1769- 1832, a French naturalist. In FIVE, Holmes remarks to Watson: 'The ideal reasoner would, when he had once been shown a single fact in all its bearings, did use from it not only all the chain of events which led up to it but also all the results which would follow from it. As Cuvier could correctly describe a whole animal by the contemplation of a single bone, so the observer who has thoroughly understood one link in a series of incidents should be able accurately to stage all the other ones, both before and after. We have not yet grasped the results which the reason alone can attain to. Problems may be solved in the study which have baffled all those who have sought a solution by the age of their senses. To carry the arts, however, to its highest page, it is necessary that the reason it should be able to utilise all the facts which have come to his knowledge, and this in itself implies, as you will readily see, a possession of all knowledge, which even in these days of free education and encyclopaedias, is a somewhat rare accomplishment.' Cuvier was a major figure in natural science research in the early 19th century and was instrumental in developing the fields of comparative anatomy and palaeontology through his work on comparison between living animals and fossils.

## DARK LANTERN

First mentioned as early as 1650, this is a lantern possessing a sliding panel which enables it to provide partial illumination.

Holmes often carried one (e.g. during the all-night vigil in REDH). Made of tin or brass, they were fuelled by signal or railroad oil. Designed and used at first solely in Britain they eventually found their way to the USA. The fluted chimney of the lantern enables the smoke to escape while the bull's eye lens concentrates the light.
Source: REDH; STUD; SIGN; GREE; WIST; EMPT; REDO; SHOS; SPEC; MILV; SIXN; BRUC; CHAS

DEDUCTION

A type of thought which begins with general principles or truths and then applies them to facts. This is the reverse of ANALYSIS which proceeds from consequences to principles.
Holmes' method was based on drawing inferences from evidence. when presented with more than one possible theory he would then choose the one that covered most of the facts. He tells Watson "It is an old maxim of mine that when you have excluded the impossible, whatever remains, however improbable, must be the truth." The principles of his theory are encapsulated in a magazine article which appears in The Book of Life (STUD):

'From a drop of water, a logician could infer the possibility of an Atlantic or a Niagara without having seen or heard of one or the other. So all life is a great chain, the nature of which is known where ever we are shown a single link of it. Like all other arts, the Science of Deduction and Analysis is one which can only be acquired by long and patient study, nor his life long enough to allow any mortal to attain the highest possible perfection in it. Before turning to those moral and mental aspects of the matter which presents the greatest difficulties, let the enquirer begin by mastering more elementary problems. Let him, on meeting a fellow mortal, learn at a glance to distinguish the history of the man and trade or profession to which he belongs. Puerile as such an exercise may seem, it sharpens the faculties of observation, and teaches one where to look and what to look for. By a man's fingernails, by his coat sleeve, by his boot, by his trouser knees, by the callosities of his forefinger and thumb, by his expression, by his shirt cuffs – by each of these things are a man's calling plainly revealed.'

On reading this document, Watson is deeply sceptical, but after he has seen Holmes in action and observed his method, he declares that "you have brought detection as near an exact science as it ever will be brought in this world."

Holmes claimed that the unobservant public did not care about the finer points of analysis and deduction (COPP). He also noted that his brother Mycroft possessed these faculties in a more advanced form then he did (BRUC).

## DE QUINCEY, THOMAS

(1785-1859) Author of Confessions of An English Opium Eater and English Romantic.

It has been suggested that Holmes may have been slightly consumptive as a youth. The lean figure, coupled with a pale, ascetic countenance, would seem to confirm this view. De Quincey explains in the "Opium Eater" how his own tendencies towards consumption were undoubtedly checked by the use of the drug opium:

".. I offered at the first glance, to a medical eye, every symptom of pthisis broadly and conspicuously developed. The hectic colours on the face, the nocturnal perspirations, the growing embarrassment of the respiration, and other expressions of growing feebleness under any attempts at taking exercise - all these symptoms were accumulating between the age of twenty two and twenty four. What was it that first arrested them ? Simply the use of opium."

There is another theory, and one that conforms to the
personality of the detective. Holmes, as I have demonstrated
elsewhere  (in *Sherlock And Porlock* )was preoccupied with
German Romanticism in his earlier years. Goethe was his guiding
light, Richter his great love. Thomas Carlyle came into the
picture as the supreme interpreter of these two thinkers.
All three writers posited a world picture in which material
ambitions and demonstrations came second. They emphasised not
the body but the soul. It was an extremely subjective view of
Man's nature which held that an individual might achieve the
heights of sublimity if he chose the correct path. Nature, of
course, was the divine inspiration and Holmes identified with this
point of view. But the English interpreters of the German school
took this one stage further. They produced a heady kind of
mysticism. The imagination, they claimed, was what was most
important, for this was Man's greatest gift. And the emphasis on
the imagination led them inevitably into the region of visions and
dreams.
With some of these writers, drugs were of no consequence.
Wordsworth, for example, was sufficiently "high" and did not
resort to them. Blake also was a natural visionary. But with other,
more earth-bound mortals the drugs did become important. This
is why Coleridge and De Quincey form such fascinating parallels.
To Coleridge the drug laudanum was a hindrance but it also
provided a release he required to allow his imagination to roam
unfettered. To De Quincey the drug opium provided a welcome
heightening of his awareness.
With Holmes, too, drugs were a way of assisting his mental
faculties. "My mind is like a racing engine," he claimed, tearing
itself to pieces because it is not connected up with the work for
which it was built." Cocaine and morphine provided the perfect
solution; cocaine is an "upper", morphine a "downer." With these

51

two drugs at his disposal, Holmes could regulate his won metabolism, pushing it beyond normal bounds. Instances of extraordinary activity contrast sharply with those of great langour. Compare these two passages, for example:

" See the fox hound with hanging ears and drooping tail... and compare it with the same hound as, with gleaming eyes and straining muscles, it runs upon a breast-high scent. Such was the change in Holmes since the morning."

"Holmes had spent several days in bed, as was his habit from time to time..."

Holmes did not have the situation as such under control as he would have liked. What he was probably aiming for with the morphine was a slowing down of his metabolism, a continuum. De Quincey again:

.. whereas wine disorders the mental faculties, opium introduces amongst them the most exquisite order, legislation and harmony... it communicates serenity and equipoise to all the faculties..."

De Quincey abjured the use of alcohol. We note also that Holmes was no great user of the drug. No doubt its unwelcome side effects left much to be desired. Morphine is far more predictable.
But there are other parallels to be drawn between Holmes and the Romantics. The effects of the opiates is to induce a desire for isolation. Coleridge sought refuge in the lonely farmhouse near Porlock. De Quincey too admitted that his decision to move to Cumbria was induced by this need for separation from the common herd. "In that state," he wrote, "crowds become an oppression to him... He naturally seeks solitude and silence, as indispensable conditions of those trances, or profoundest

reveries." De Quincey moved to the Lakes in 1812 to study German metaphysics. Holmes, it appears, could achieve the same effect by retiring to the bedroom at 221B and reaching for his hypodermic.


DERBIES

(sl.) Handcuffs. '...hold out while I fix the derbies' -Athelney Jones to John Clay, REDH. The O.E.D. has the word as handcuffs from c.1660 onwards. Cf. Marryat in Japhet: "We may as well put on the darbies", continued he, producing a pair of handcuffs'. The word originates from a rigid form of usurer's bond called 'Father Dierby's' . Source: REDH

DEVIL'S FOOT ROOT

"It has not found its way either into the pharmacopoiea or into the literature of toxicology. The root is shaped like foot, half-human, half goat-like, hence the fanciful name given by a botanical missionary. It is used as an ordeal poison by the medicine men in certain districts of West Africa, and it is kept as a secret among them. This particular specimen I obtained under very extraordinary circumstances in the Ubanghi country."
-Dr Leon Sterndale, DEVI.

It was in the Spring of 1897 1 when Sherlock Holmes came face to face with one of the most bizarre cases of poisoning which he was ever to confront in his long and distinguished career. It will be recalled that, having suffered a breakdown, 2, he and Watson travelled to the remote Cornish village of Tredannack Wollas, near Poldhu Bay. It was here that the obscure and deadly "Devil's Foot" killed two people and drove two others to insanity. 3
This poison had been taken from the possessions of Dr Leon

Sterndale, the explorer, to enable Mortimer to destroy his sister Brenda Tregennis. As Dr Sterndale relates, the drug was kept among his African mementoes,for he had obtained it whilst on an expedition in West Africa.

"One day, only a couple of weeks ago, he came down to my cottage and I showed him some of my African curiosities. Among other things I exhibited this powder, and I told him of its strange properties, how it stimulates those brain centres which control the emotion of fear, and how either madness or death is the fate of the unhappy native who is subjected to the ordeal by the priest of his tribe. I told him also how powerless European science would be to detect it. How he took it I cannot say, for I never left the room, but there is no doubt that it was then, while I was opening cabinets and stooping to boxes, that he managed to abstract some of the devil's foot root."

What precisely was this poison which brought death and vengeance to a quiet corner of Cornwall ? Certainly it has not been officially listed in the pharmacopoeia under the name given it by Dr Sterndale, so we must look elsewhere for its source and identity. But before doing so, let us consider the evidence made available to us by Dr Watson.
According to Dr Sterndale, the poison otherwise called radix pedis diaboli) was virtually unknown among Western toxicologists. '... save for one sample in a laboratory in Buda, 4, there is no other specimen in Europe. It has not yet found its way into the pharmacopoeia or into the literature of toxicology. The root is shaped like a foot, half human, half goat like; hence the fanciful name given by a botanical missionary."
Dr Sterndale did not possess the poison in its original state, but produced what is described in the narrative as "a reddish-brown powder" which he claimed to have obtained "in the Ubanghi country." 5 of Western Africa.

# The Criminological Sherlock Holmes

The effects of this psycho-active drug are recorded by Dr Watson in that remarkable experiment carried out by Holmes in the Cornish cottage:

"I hardly settled in my chair before I was conscious of a thick, musky odour, subtle and nauseous. At the very first whiff of it my brain and my imagination were beyond all control. A thick, black cloud swirled before my eyes, and my mind told me that in this cloud, unseen as yet, but about to spring out upon my appalled senses, lurked all that was vaguely horrible, all that was monstrous and inconceivably wicked in the universe. Vague shapes swirled and swam amid the dark cloud-bank, each a menace and a warning of something coming, the advent of some unspeakable dweller upon the threshold, 6, whose very shadow would blast my soul. A freezing horror took possession of me. I felt that my hair was rising, that my eyes were protruding, that my mouth was opened, and my tongue like leather. The turmoil within my brain was such that something must surely snap. I tried to scream, and was vaguely aware of some hoarse croak which was my own voice, but distant and detached from myself."

The fear-inducing properties of the drug are graphically conveyed in this passage which admittedly has a great deal of literary embellishment but nevertheless conveys the essential claustrophobia of the original experience.

Clearly the term "Devil's Foot" is a convenient one, probably employed by Dr Watson because he did not wish to publicise the remarkable ability of the poison to leave no trace in the body of the deceased. Peter Cooper 7 observes that "the same title is given by the Apaches and Comanches to the peyote or mescal button; but peyote is euphoriant and produces brightness rather than blackness of vision and mood. Moreover, its provenance and setting are hopelessly at fault."

There are, however, a number of points which should lead us to the identification of radix pedis diaboli.

1. It comes from West Africa, NOT the South American continent.
2. It is pure, organic-derived poison. (Dr B. Koelle 8, has suggested lysergic acid, but the formula of this drug was not invented until 1943 in a Swiss laboratory.)
3. It is shaped like a foot and when ground up assumes a reddish-brown colour.
4. It also has a Latin name. As Verner Andersen points out 9, "Such names are usually only given to vegetable drugs when they are standardised by a description in a pharmacopoeia or a similar formulary." In other words, the poison had already been classified by western toxicologists.
5. It is a psycho-active drug, used as an ordeal poison. These drugs have been thoroughly investigated by western observers and by the 1890's considerable documentation had been made of their varieties. In fact, as Andersen demonstrates, 9, the only drug mentioned in the British Pharmacopoeia of 1885 (the volume which would have been available to Dr Watson) that originates from the Ubanghi area of West Africa is the dried seed of the Physostigma Venenosum, otherwise known as the Calabar Bean. However, before any concrete decision is made about the Calabar Bean, let us examine the other possible contenders.
The first of these is Datura stramonium, offered to us as a possibility by Peter Cooper 7, (otherwise known as L'Herbe au Diable, or thornapple.) This plant contains active principles similar to those found in atropa belladonna (deadly nightshade.). The active principal constituents are atropine and hyoscine. Datura has a distinguished history and was purported to have been employed by the Delphic oracle.10
Datura Stramonium was also used extensively in the Middle Ages by Italian poisoners who developed a brew which instantly deadened the senses of the victim.

In India it was rumoured that Hindu prostitutes gave their clients Datura so as to render them unconscious for long periods of time. Considering the nature of their occupation, this seems a very practical method of dampening male ardour.

During the late 18th Century white slave traders administered a concoction of aphrodisiacs and Datura to their victim. When they awoke, their virginity and all memory of their experience had disappeared.

Datura contains three active alkaloids: atropine, scopolamine and hyoscyamine. Both atropine and scopolamine are extremely dangerous drugs, so much so that their dosage is recommended only between 1/500 and 1/100 of a grain. And both have a direct effect on the central nervous systems, causing a disruption in mental association. As one early writer described its effects:

"He who partakes of it is deprived of his reason; for a long time laughing or weeping, or sleeping and often times talking and replying, so that at times he appears to be in his right mind, but really being out of it and not knowing to whom he is speaking, nor remembering what has happened after his alienation has passed."

The one factor which casts doubt upon the identification of Datura as the Devil's Foot is that it induces vomiting when administered orally, as Peter Cooper correctly observes, 7, and it is unlikely that it would have the effects observed by Holmes and Watson when absorbed through the lungs.

Peter Cooper 7 suggests the ordeal drug known as muavi (Erythrpleum guineense) which was popular among witch doctors in the Congo region. His main reason for this suggestion appears to be that Doyle himself travelled to West Africa in 1881 where he "penetrated above Old Calabar into the mangrove swamps." 11 Another claim has been made by F.A. Allen, 12, who prefers reserpine in the shape of Rauwolfia vomitoria.This is a shrub that grew in abundance in the Belgian Congo at one time but it was of such a height (eighteen feet) that harvesting it became uneconomic. The relatives of rauwolfia vomitoria (rauwolfia serpentina, rauwolfia tetraphylla, etc.) have provided the main source of reserpine which is now produced synthetically as a sedative and tranquillizer. 13 It seems unlikely that this drug provided the source of the Devil's Foot since, like Datura, it is usually administered orally and causes severe vomiting.

Another contender is hemp. Since this drug is smoked like tobacco, it is a distinct possibility.

As Peter Cooper observes 7, Du Chaillu, the explorer, noted hemp smoking among the Ashira and Apingi of the Congo as long ago as 1861. "Practised smokers are soon laughing, talking, quarrelling and acting in all respects like drunken persons. Insanity is often its ultimate result on those who persist in its use."

Hemp is of course a psycho-active drug, and an extremely vivid account of its effects on the user was made by Theophile Gautier in 1843. 14 He records:

"After several minutes a sense of numbness overwhelmed me. It seemed that my body had dissolved and become transparent. I saw very clearly inside me the hashish I had eaten in the form of an emerald which radiated millions of tiny sparks... All around me I heard the shattering and crumbling of jewels of all colours; songs renewed themselves without ceasing as in the play of a kaleidoscope. At certain moments I still saw my comrades, but disfigured and grotesque, half men, half plants."

It is interesting to note that at first the user experiences disembodiment. Then both his sight and hearing are affected and distorted. As Harold Burn remarks, 15, there is a close link between the effects of hashish and those of mescaline.

Let us now return to the Calabar Bean, otherwise known as

Physostigmatis Semen, the dried seed of Physostigma Venenosum.

The plant was first discovered by the Reverend W.C. Thompson who in 1859 sent some flowering specimens to Professor J. H. Balfour of Edinburgh. 16 It was Balfour who in 1860 gave the plant its Latin name, but it was Robert Christison who first demonstrated its toxic effects. 17

The Physostigma venenosum contains an active ingredient known as physistigmine. It is used mainly as a treatment for glaucoma and reduces the pressure experienced inside the eyeball. Among the chiefs of the Calabar region, however, the plant was considered to be sacred and it was closely guarded until the time of the rituals.

Several hundred people were killed each year during the rituals which were attended by the King and his principal courtiers. The victims, most of whom were convicted of witchcraft, were forced to chew the beans. If they vomited these up they were declared innocent but usually they died within half an hour of taking the poison. The drug caused intense thirst and as the victim's saliva increased, his stomach and respiratory tract filled with fluid, causing him to slowly drown.

The bean itself is kidney shaped and about the size of a pigeon's egg. It has a hard, shiny, chocolate coloured shell and when ground up, produces a substance similar to the "reddish-brown, snuff-like powder" mentioned in DEVI.

The experiments conducted by Thomas R. Fraser, and recorded in his paper 18 on the subject, describe the effects of both a small and large does of the poison on one of the lower animals.

With the smaller dose, Fraser observed firstly a slight tremor, "extending from the hindquarters to the forelimbs and head." This was followed by both paralysis and flaccidity of the musculature. The rectum and bladder were then emptied, the pupils contracted, the breathing became slow and irregular and a frothy mucus escaped from the mouth. After a succession of muscular contractions, death coincided with respiratory failure. The large dose caused the animal to collapse, its hind legs paralysed. After the contraction of the pupils, respiration ceased and death followed.

Sir Robert Christison's experiments 19, were carried out in 1855 and, like many toxicologists of the period, he was himself the guinea pig. The dose he administered was short of poisonous. Twelve grains of the seed, chewed, then swallowed, acted in twenty minutes, causing giddiness and sleepiness. After emptying his stomach forcibly, he discovered that the giddiness continued. His pulse slowed down though his mental faculties remained intact, and he eventually fell into a deep sleep.

In the summer of 1864, 70 children from Liverpool ate a quantity of calabar beans which they found among the rubbish thrown out by the ship Commodore. They were treated at the Southern Hospital. One six year old, who had eaten six beans, died after severe abdominal pain, vomiting, muscular prostration, staggering gait and contracted pupils.

As the chemistry lecturer J Baker Edwards observed after examining the body, "In criminal cases, nothing might be detected by autopsy or by chemical analysis to reveal the cause of death." 20

The muscular paralysis the bean produces is caused by its action on the spinal cord, although it has the effect of first relaxing the musculature. It also has an unusual effect on the heart, tending to cause stoppage in the state of diastole.

The problem with the calabar bean as a contender for the Devil's Foot is that it does not cause the hallucinations recorded by Dr Watson. It is more than possible, however, that the good doctor changed the details of the effects of the drug simply to dissuade the criminal fraternity from using it. Having read Edwards' notes on the subject, he would have been aware of its effects and the impossibility of pathologists proving the cause of death. Having witnessed events at Tredannack Wollas he would have trod a careful course when publicising the tragedy. 21

1. Dr Watson, DEVI
2. Holmes suffered from manic depression.
3. Brenda and Mortimer Tregennis died: Owen and George went mad.
4. Buda - Pesth or Budapest, capital of Hungary.
5. Part of French equatorial Africa. This eastern colony, lying North of the Belgian Congo and East of Sudan, derives its names from two rivers, the Ubangi and the Shari, which flow into the Chad. Although cotton is the chief export, the area was until recently, virtually untapped. It covers an area of 238, 767 square miles.
6. A phrase H.P. Lovecraft, the American fantasist, was to adapt as a title of one of his supernatural collections.
7. "The Devil's Foot - An Excursion Into Holmesian Toxicology", SHJ
8. "Leaves From The Copper Beeches", 1958. Dr Koelle was head of the toxicological department of the well-known Swiss pharmaceutical firm of Sandoz.
9. Radix Pedis Diabolis, SHJ, Winter 1975, pp. 54 - 55.
10. The Priestess of the God (called the Pythia) sat on a tripod over a crack in the rock and uttered words in her divine trance. These were then interpreted by another in the form of verses.
11. Doctor Varro E. Tyler,Professor of Pharmacology at Purdue University, Indiana, disagrees. He prefers niando, also used by the Congo natives, mainly as an intoxicant. See SHJ, Vol 8, No. 2, p.61.
12. M & B Pharmaceutical Bulletin 5, 1956, p. 118.
13. Rauwolfia as a genus of plants was named by Charles Plumier in 1703. It comprises over eighty varieties of plant.
14. Le Club des Hachichins.
15. "Drugs, Medicines And Man", p. 209

16. See Verner Andersen's Radix Pedis Diabolis, SHJ, Winter 1975, p.55.

17. Reprinted in "Two Hundred Years of Materia Medica at Edinburgh, 1968."

18. "On The Physiological Action Of The Calabar Bean" - Trans. Royal Society, Edinburgh, Vol 24, 1867.

19. See Sherlock Holmes And Poisons..

20. Notes on the cases of Poisoning by Calabar Beans in Liverpool", Pharm. Journal, 1864, - 65, p.99

21. This is Verner Andersen's contention.

DISGUISE

Disguise is frequently alluded to in the Sherlock Holmes stories. Holmes is a master of disguise and often shows his abilities when he is in pursuit of a criminal. Watson often describes the detectives abilities, as in this description in SCAN:

'It was close upon four before the door opened and a drunken looking groom, ill-kempt and side whiskered, with an inflamed face and disreputable clothes, walked into the room. Accustomed as I was to my friends amazing powers in the use of disguises, I had to look three times before I was certain that it was indeed he.'

Holmes was able not only to change his physical appearance but to project different personalities according to the roles that he adopted:

'It was not merely that Holmes changed his costume. His expression, his manner, his very soul seemed to vary with every fresh part that he assumed.'

In his long career, Holmes adopted the following disguises: a blue blouse to portray a French plumber in LADY, a tourist in HOUN, a black robe and hat to become an Italian priest in FINA, and a pea coat in SIGN which Watson describes as 'old' and 'buttoned up to his throat.' Holmes also used a wig and fake whiskers and eyebrows to complete his sailor disguise. In FINA, he becomes an aged bookseller with a wrinkled face, a protruding lower lip and a stoop. His most elaborate transformation was that of an Irish-American traitor called Altamont in LAST where his voice was enough to convince the Germans of his authenticity. Hans Gross, the Austrian criminologist, in his seminal work, *Criminal Investigation*, published in Britain in 1907, stresses the importance of disguise amongst criminals and warns investigators to be aware of the existence of false scars limps and several other deformities since criminals often use these tricks to their advantage:

'Criminals have constantly recourse to disguises. With what cleverness and persistency they keep on disguising themselves, and yet it is not superfluous to urge attention to the matter ; for indeed there is nothing which malefactors will not try to simulate, nothing they will not try to dissimulate. Frequently the medical man alone can decide whether or not there be dissimulation, and it will be the business of the Investigating Officer to place no faith in pretended infirmities and maladies,
and to call in regularly the advice of the medical man.
But here again there are numerous cases where it is impossible to fall back upon the medical man ; it may be the nature of the affair excludes medical assistance or, it may be, an important decision must be come to before being able to call in the aid of the physician.'

The use of disguise is well illustrated in TWIS where Neville St Clair, a respectable middle-class businessman discovers that it is more profitable to disguise himself as a beggar. Gross quotes a case of a man who established a successful career as a beggar,

appearing to be blind, a condition he simulated by putting drops
of erserine into his eyes, causing the pupils to contract.


## DISTRICT MESSENGER

An employee of the District Messenger Service Company which
used an express delivery service throughout London and the
suburbs. The rates charged were twice as expensive as those of
the General Post Office. Holmes used the services of a district
messenger to communicate with Baron Gruner. He also
visited the district messenger offices in HOUN. Source: ILLU;
HOUN, Ch.4

## DOGS

Although dogs were not widely used during the late Victorian
period in crime detection, Holmes was the exception. Several
dogs appear in the Holmes saga: the small terrier which Holmes
subjects to an experiment in STUD, the Spaniel belonging to
Lady Beatrice Falder in SHOS, and the nameless hound in SILV,
who famously did nothing in the night-time. In the later case of
the Canon, CREE, we discover that Holmes had considered
writing a monograph on the use of dogs in detective work. In
SIGN, Holmes instructs Watson to fetch Toby who is described as
'half Spaniel and half lurcher.' This hound he uses to track Tonga
who has trodden in creosote. Unfortunately for the dog Toby
leads Watson to a creosote factory. Nevertheless, Holmes has
high hopes for Toby. In CREE, Holmes extols the virtues of dogs
and bases his analysis of Professor Presbury's strange behaviour
on the behaviour of his dog. The attack on the Prof by his pet dog
Roy almost leads to disaster, an event which is similar to the
attack on the infamous Jephro Rucastle when his mastiff Carlo

attacks and almost kills him. (COPP) In MISS, Holmes utilises a part foxhound and beagle called Pompey in order to help find Godfrey Staunton. Holmes uses a syringe to squirt aniseed oil onto one of the wheels of Dr Armstrong's carriage. Pompey pursues the aniseed odour, ending up at the cottage where Staunton is discovered with his dead wife.

## DRAGHOUNDS

Hounds trained to pursue an artificial scent instead of that of a wild animal. Pompey was the 'pride of the local drag hounds'. Cf. The Times, 4 February 8/2 (1884): '...heading the Household Brigade Drag Hounds...'
Source: MISS

## DROPSY

A disease characterised by an accumulation of watery fluid in the cavities of the patient's body. Lord Norberton's sister died of this disease. The O.E.D. has the word as early as c.1290, regarding it as an aphetic form of the M.E. 'ydropsy'. (Otherwise hydropsy)
Source: SHOS

## DRUGS

See COCAINE, MORPHINE, OPIUM, LAUDANUM

## DYSPNOEA

(Gr. dyspnoia: des - ill; pnoea - breathing) Difficulty in breathing, caused by a weak heart. Sir Charles Baskerville suffered from this condition. Cf. The Lancet 27 Sept, 1890, 663/2: 'Obesity develops.. .so that the least exertion will produce dyspnoea'.
Source: HOUN, Ch.2

ELEPHANT GUN

A large-bore shotgun employed in the hunting of elephants.
Godfrey Emsworth was hit by a bullet from an elephant gun.
Source: BLAN

ELEY'S NO.2

A Webley's No.2; a small pocket pistol which took Eley.320
cartridges. Holmes suggested Watson take his 'Eley's No.2' with
him to Stoke Moran. Source: SPEC

EPITHELIAL SCALES

(Mod.L.: Gr. - upon; thele - nipple) Scales of the outer tissue of
the skin, often pertaining to the mucous membranes of animals.
In this case, flakes of dandruff. Holmes examined these through a
low power microscope at the beginning of SHOS. Cf. Mivart's
Elementary Anatomy (1872) p.237. Source: SHOS

ERYSIPELAS

(Of doubtful etymology. Commonly regarded as EPVOI-S. An
inflammatory disease, the face, reddening, generally marked by a
bright redness of the skin and often named 'St Anthony's Fire'.
Holmes was rumoured to have suffered this condition after his
attack by Baron Gruner's thugs. Source: ILLU

ETHER

(Injected) (L. aether: Gr. aither, the heavens) An anaesthetic given
to Lady Frances Carfax to help her condition. Now frowned on
by the medical profession in cases such as this.

Source: LADY

## EXPANDED REVOLVER BULLET

Otherwise known as a 'dum-dum' bullet, and so named because it was first made at Dum Dum, near Calcutta. The soft-nosed bullet mushrooms out when it makes impact, thus causing extensive wounding. Ronald Adair fell victim to a dumdum bullet fired from Colonel Sebastien Moran's air-gun.

## EXTRAVASATED

(L. extra - outside; vas - vessel) Split, disseminated. An examination of McPherson's body revealed a number of dots showing 'extravasated blood'. Cf. MacCormac, Antiseptic Surgery, (1880) p.103: 'Blood is extravasated into the tissues'. Source: LION

## FELONY

(O.Fr: L.L. fello-onis, a traitor) A crime (including burglary and murder) more serious than a misdemeanour but less serious than treason.The distinction between a felony and a misdemeanour no longer exists. Holmes used the term in referring to James Ryder. Source: BLUE; 3GAB; BRUC

## FENCE

(sl. Aphetic, from defence)    A receiver of stolen property. Shinwell Johnson uses the term. Source: ILLU

## FINGERPRINTS

An impression made by a fingertip. Each fingerprint is unique and the properties of skin furrows do not change during a person's life. When fingerprints are clear it is a simple task to identify matching finger impressions. The first system of fingerprint identification was devised by Francis Galton in 1892 in his influential book entitled Fingerprints, although the idea was not adopted by Scotland Yard until as late as 1901. By 1910, this system had been adopted throughout Europe. Fingerprints are referred to in seven of the sixty Holmes stories, and Holmes shows himself to be a pioneer in this area as early as 1894, in the case of The Norwood Builder when he proves that the police have been duped by a print falsely planted in order to incriminate an innocent person, John Hector McFarlane.  It is possible that the thumbprint idea in The Norwood Builder was derived from an article in the June 27, 1903 edition of the magazine Titbits in an article entitled *Criminals Convict Themselves*. This describes a case in Yorkshire where a burglar left a dirty thumbprint in a book he had examined. The earliest use of fingerprint identification in The Canon can be found in SIGN, where Holmes notes a thumb mark on an envelope sent by Thaddeus Sholto to  Mary Morstan which Holmes ascribes to that of a postman. In TWIS, he notices a greasy thumbprint on an envelope containing a note from Neville Sinclair to his wife. In CARD, he sees two distinctive thumb marks on a cardboard box containing two ears, sent by Jim Brown to Susan Cushing.


FOOTSTEPS

Also footprints. The impression left by a foot. In STUD Holmes claimed there was no branch of detection which was so important and so neglected as the art of tracing footsteps. He also wrote a monograph on the subject. (see Appendix Two.) Footprints are mentioned in 26 of the 60 cases and they appear in a variety of materials, including snow, (BERY) on a carpet (RESI), mud

(SIGN), a curtain (CROO) and ash (GOLD). In the first two stories, STUD and SIGN, Holmes is able to trace his targets and in SIGN his task is made that much easier by the fact that Tonga, a pygmy from the Andaman Islands, has a diminutive foot whilst his companion has a peg leg. In BERY, four people leave their footprints in the snow, fast revealing what Holmes describes as a 'very long and complex story... in front of me.' The concept of running footprints is well delineated in HOUN where Holmes is able to deduce from the footprints of Sir Charles Baskerville that he was running for his life and not as had been suggested, merely tiptoeing. One of Holmes's most dazzling demonstrations is shown in RESI, where he astounds Watson by using footprints on the carpet to indicate the presence of Mr Blessington's murderers. In BOSC, Holmes relies on footprints almost exclusively in order to solve the case and takes great care in examining footprints at the scene of crime, having to exclude the footprints of a number of visitors to the scene including those of Inspector Lestrade. During the course of his long career, Holmes became so expert at reading footprints that in a much later case, WIST, he is able to know the size of the print merely by glancing at it. The intrepid Austrian judge and criminologist Hans Gross, in his *Criminal Investigation*, published in 1907 in Britain, devotes an entire section of his work to the reading and recording of footprints. There is every likelihood that Holmes would have used this pioneering work. His introduction to the section on footprints is distinctly Holmesian in manner:

'Whoever desires to commence the study of footprints upon the scene of the crime will discover practically nothing at all. A footprint is an impression, in a sense like all other impressions but in fact very different from them. And in addition it is not always well defined and when it is defined one cannot take it away with one ; even if one could, it would be impossible to search the whole town and make experiments with every citizen to see if he is the author of the crime. These considerations detract. from the value of footprints. One must learn how to see, and one cannot learn how to see without practising. What does an outsider see through a microscope ? What does a huntsman see or hear in the field and the forest when all seems dead to another? What does the artist see in a picture which is to an unartistic person but an assemblage of coloured figures? What is wearisome chaos to a beginner is a world full of life and ideas to the man who knows. A few footprints do not amount to much, but to the Investigating Officer they may mean everything, upon them may depend the success of his work  the salvation of an innocent and the conviction of a guilty person. One senses that this microcosm which leaves these prints is not wanting in importance. Here, again, the Investigating Officer must unite his observations in a sympathetic whole. It does not suffice to look at large numbers of footprints; by only looking at them no order can be given to his ideas, nothing will be retained, nothing will be grouped, and the utility of what may have been seen will, through seeing too much, be nil. To be able to obtain some advantage from these studies, one may commence by considering attentively, and following, for example on a dusty road, the impressions of the feet of small and big persons, of boots and bare feet, of the footprints of animals, and the wheels of vehicles intermingled confusedly.'

## FORGERY

In law, the fraudulent making of alterations of writing or instrument to the prejudice of another man's rights. In STUD, Lestrade consults Holmes in a forgery case whilst in SIXN, Holmes investigates the Conk Singleton forgery case. ( see entry) He also believed that Professor Moriarty was involved in a number of cases of this sort (FINA, VALL).

## FLY PAPER

Brown paper, impregnated with arsenic and used as a method by which to kill flies (popular in Victorian times and also sometimes used as a method of murder). The message which struck Victor Trevor's father dead made reference to supplies of fly paper. Source: GLOR

## FORMOSA CORRUPTION (BLACK)

An invented disease, referred to by Holmes in DYIN. Formosa is an island off the south-east coast of China. Source: DYIN

## FOWLING-PIECE

Shotgun (so named because these guns were used to shoot wild fowl). The murder weapon in VALL was a fowling-piece. Cf, G. Bird, Nat.Phil, p130 (1839): '...the well-known double report of a fowling-piece, fired at a distance'. Source: VALL, Ch.7

## FULLER'S EARTH

(As early as 1523, O.Fr. fuler and O.E. fullere, fuller) A sandy clay used for industrial and medical purposes. The earthy, hydrous aluminium silicate, of which it is composed, is ideal for the absorption of grease. Colonel Lysander Stark claimed to be mining fullers earth at Eyford. Source: ENGR

## GARROTTER

(From garotte, a Spanish method of putting criminals to death.) A criminal who strangles his victims with a piece of knotted cord prior to robbing them. This was a popular method in Victorian London. Parker, who watched Holmes' apartments in Baker Street, was a garrotter. Cf. Law Times (1885), 14 Mar, 348/1:

"Lord Bramwell...sentenced many a garrotter to his cat'.Source: EMPT

## GAS

Josiah Amberley murdered his wife and her lover by suffocating them with the poisonous effects of coal gas inhalation (RETI).

## GEOLOGY

Watson (STUD) rated Holmes' knowledge of geology as 'practical but limited'. However, elsewhere, (FIVE, SIGN, STUD), Holmes was able to tell at a glance different types of soil from one another.

## GUAIACUM TEST, THE OLD

An old and 'unreliable' (Holmes' word) blood test which used to be carried out by criminologists, involving resin from the guaiacum tree. A stain would turn blue if blood were present. The Guaiacum tree is native to the West Indies and South America. Source: STUD, Ch.1

## HAEMOGLOBIN

A substance found in the red corpuscles of blood. Holmes believed he had discovered a reagent which was precipitated by haemoglobin and by nothing else (STUD).

## HAIR-TRIGGER

(From 1830 onwards) A secondary trigger which releases the main trigger by slight pressure. Holmes possessed a revolver with a hair trigger. Cf. T. Hook, G. Gurney 2, 192: 'My pistol, which had the hair-trigger set, went off'. Also cf. the official catalogue of The Great Exhibition, p353: 'Double rifle, with single hair-trigger'.

## HANDWRITING

Holmes was a keen student of handwriting and claimed that being able to deduce a man's age and personality from his writing was a science which had been brought to some accuracy by experts in the field (REDC), a claim which for the time was not always shared by other criminologists, Hans Gross and Alexander Cargill being the exceptions to this. Doubts had been cast over the reputation of Alphonse Bertillon when in 1892 he used handwriting analysis to pronounce that Dreyfus had written a controversial memorandum. Cargill published an article entitled *Health and Handwriting* in 1890 in which he claimed that handwriting could be used to determine age, character and perhaps gender. Interestingly, he sent a copy of the article to Conan Doyle in December 1892, a year before the publication of The Reigate Squires. Holmes used handwriting analysis in no less than nine of the cases investigated, the first example being that of a letter received by Miss Mary Morstan in SIGN. He also was able to make deductions about the date of an ancient manuscript in HOUN based on the style of writing and he analysed the writing in the will made by Jonas Oldacre in NORW. In the case of the Reigate Squires, he examined the fragment of a note sent by the Cunninghams to William Kirwin. In The Red Circle, Cargill's claim about gender and handwriting is borne out. In the story, Emilia, the hidden lodger, sends printed messages to her landlady in an effort to conceal her gender because she has replaced the original tenant, her husband Gennaro. Holmes, using his knowledge of handwriting analysis, deduces what is actually going on.

## HOLMES, METHODS

Holmes' methods were a combination of instinct and observation. He pioneered the business of crime scene investigation and deductive reasoning. Even as a college student, he had already formed into a system certain habits of observation and inference which would play an important part in his life (GLOR) and elsewhere admitted that his methods were based on a mixture of imagination and reality (THOR). He further defined his method as consisting of a combination of three elements: the power of observation, the power of deduction and a wide range of exact knowledge (SIGN). He told Watson that his deductions were based on the solid and minute examination of evidence (BOSC) and elsewhere claimed that 'there is nothing so important as trifles.'
He was also very critical of other people's efforts to apply his own methods, observing that 'you see but you do not observe.' (SCAN). As regards his method of deduction (see DEDUCTION), he noted that 'The more outré and grotesque and incident is, the more carefully it deserves to be examined, and the very point which appears to complicated a case is, when duly considered and scientifically handled, the one which is most likely to elucidate it.' (HOUN) He also observed that 'As a rule, the more bizarre a thing is the less mysterious it proves to be.' (REDH) His most famous maxim was: 'When you have eliminated the impossible, whatever remains, however improbable, must be the truth.' Holmes also used his vast knowledge to recognise clues that other people might miss and was able to distinguish between various methods of death, meticulously analysing the evidence that he found including evidence of bloodstains, the tracing of footsteps, handwriting

analysis and firearm residues. He also paid attention to very subtle clues which might for example be dependent on tobacco ash, cigarette butts and even odours. He relied upon a wide and diverse source of knowledge to assist him in his investigations and observed that 'The interplay of ideas and the oblique uses of knowledge are often of extraordinary interest.' (VALL) noting that he had a 'passion for definite and exact knowledge.' (SCAN) He told Watson that his mind was like a crowded box room with packets of all sorts stowed away therein, 'so many that I may well have but a vague perception of what was there.' (LION) To assist him in his endeavours he kept a library of works including the American Encyclopaedia, Bradshaw, a medical directory and an encyclopaedia of reference, along with two gazetteers and his commonplace book.

## HOOLIGAN

A street rough; a young violent person, said to be the name of a leader of a gang, possibly Hooley's gang, a family resident in the mid 1890's in Islington (W. Ware). The alternative theory is that the word derives from the Houlihans, an Irish family resident in the Borough (London). Is there a link though with the Hindi Hoolee, hoili - that great festival held at the vernal equinox? Source: REDC

## HORSE FAKER

A person who conceals the identity of a horse by dyeing its coat and mane. Holmes suspected Silas Brown of being one. Partridge has: horse dealer - low (1887). Cf. Baumann: horse- capper. Source: SILV

## HOTTENTOT

A Dutch imitative word approximating to the S.W. Africa khoi-
khoin - men of men) One of a dwindling, nomadic, pastoral, pale-
brown-skinned race of S.W. Africa resembling the Bushmen and
the Bantu: also, a barbarian or a coloured person (derogatory).
The Hottentots were all but exterminated by the Boer settlers. Dr
Mortimer and Sir Charles Baskerville spent 'many a charming
evening' discussing the comparative anatomy of the Hottentot and
the Bushman, a discussion which one commentator has suggested
might have centred upon their pronounced buttocks, a condition
classified as steatopygia. (modified L. from STEARIN (fat) and
Gk. puge, rump) The excessive development of fat on the
buttocks of the Hottentot and Bushman drew considerable
comment from Victorian ethnographers, who considered their
easy means of sexual intercourse abnormal. Source: HOUN

HYDROCARBONS

(Coined by Cavendish (1766) from Gr. hydor, water) A
compound of hydrogen and carbon with nothing else, occurring
chiefly in oil, natural gas and coal.   The analysis of carbon
compounds from the mid 1860's onwards led to a number of
commercial applications at the turn of the century. Holmes
succeeded in 'dissolving' a hydrocarbon (SIGN) and later
continued research into coal-tar derivatives at Montpellier.
Source: SIGN

HYPODERMIC SYRINGE

(Gr. hypo - under; dermis - skin) A syringe equipped with a fine
hollow needle. Holmes possessed one. Source: CREE; SIGN,
Ch.l.

HURET the Boulevard Assassin (1894)

Watson refers to "the tracking and arresting of Huret, the Boulevard assassin," an exploit which won for Holmes an autographed letter of thanks from the French President and the Order of the Legion of Honour". (GOLD) It was the late Edgar W. Smith who pointed out (BSJ Vol 9 No. I) that in 1894 the President of France (Marie Francois Sadi Carnot) was assassinated by one Giovanni Santo, a known Nihilist. As Chris Redmond pointed out (SHJ Vol 7 No. 4) Santo "insisted that he had no accomplices". Officials were convinced otherwise. Shortly after the assassination, M. Goron, the head of the detective force, was removed from his post because of "financial irregularities." Mr. Redmond's contention is that Holmes carried out "an investigation of the whole affair and some reforms... When Holmes was finished with it, he certainly deserved the Legion of Honour...."

## LAUDANUM

A fluid prepared from opium and a common ingredient in several Victorian patent medicines. Isa Whitney (TWIS) first became addicted to opium by drenching his tobacco with it.
Laudanum was the most common preparation of opium; also a mixture known as Godfrey's cordial which was given as a sleeping draught to infants and young children (more than half of these children were under one year of age.) Powders and pills containing opium were legion. There was Dover's powder, kino powder, a lead and opium pill (lead was not known to be harmful at the time), opium lozenges, an ipecacuanha and squill pill and many others, including an enema preparation for cases of severe constipation. See also MORPHINE and OPIUM.

## ICTHYOSIS

(Gr. ichthys, fish) Sometimes called 'fish-skin disease'. A

condition in which the sufferer's skin takes on a whitened, sealy aspect. Similar to leprosy but without the long term effects. Godfrey Emsworth suffered from the disease.
Source: BLAN


## IDEE FIXE

(Fr.) A fixed idea; a monomania. See MONOMANIA. Source: SIXN

## INQUISITION OF SEVILLE

An ecclesiastical tribunal formed for the suppression of heresy and the punishment of heretics, organized in the 13th Century under Pope Innocent 3. The Seville Inquisition, which lasted until early in the 19th Century, was responsible for the deaths of thousands of people. Watson likens the machinery of the Mormons (rather unkindly) to that of the Spanish Inquisition.
Source: STUD, Pt.2, Ch.3

## IODOFORM

(Gr. ioeides, violet-coloured, eidos, form)    A compound of iodine, used as an antiseptic and analogous to chloroform, Watson smelled of iodoform when he walked into Holmes' rooms.Source: SCAN

## JEMMY

(Partridge has this as 1811. By 1870 the term was colloquial. A common variant is jimmy) A crowbar used by burglars.
Source: NAVA; CHAS; SHOS; 3GAR; BRUC

## JEZAIL (BULLET)

East Indian, 1838 (Urdu: jazail) A bullet fired from a long Afghan musket. The bullet which shattered Watson's shoulder bone and grazed his subclavian artery would have been compounded of nails and fragments of silver. Its extraction might have proved extremely difficult. Source: STUD, Ch.1; NOBL

## LANGUR

(Hindi, lagur) The entellus monkey or other of its genus (presbytis entellus). It is a brightly coloured creature with crests of hair on its head and contrasting patches of naked skin. The entellus male normally weighs 20-30lb, but in the Himalayas, where it ranges up to 10,000ft, it can grow even bigger. Langurs are extremely intelligent creatures with a highly developed social order. It is highly likely that the 'serum of anthropoid' which Professor Presbury administered to himself (CREE) and which was taken from this 'black-faced monkey of the Himalayan slopes' may have been chosen because of the humanoid qualities of the langur.
Source: CREE

## LASCAR

An East-Indian sailor (from the Urdu and Persian laskar – army O.E.D.) A 'rascally Lascar' ran the opium den in Upper Swandam Lane. Source: TWIS

## LAUDANUM

(Coined by Paracelsus: perhaps ladanum, transferred to a different drug) An alcoholic preparation of opium in liquid form, commonly administered as a pain reliever in Victorian times.

S.T.Coleridge and De Quincey became addicted to it; among others Isa Whitney (TWIS) became addicted to opium through using laudanum. Laudanum was the commonest preparation of opium; also a mixture known as Godfrey's cordial which was given as a sleeping draught to infants and young children (more than half of these children were under one year of age.) Powders and pills containing opium were legion. There was Dover's powder, kino powder, a lead and opium pill (lead was not known to be harmful at the time), opium lozenges, an ipecacuanha and squill pill and many others, including an enema preparation for cases of severe constipation.

## LECOQ

A detective, invented by Emile Gaboriau. He first appeared in the detective novel entitled the fair L'Affaire Rouge in 1866 and was introduced as an amateur detective. The character of the novel was based on a real-life thief turned police officer, Eugene François Vidocq whose own memoirs, Les Vrais Memoires De Vidocq, mixed fiction and fact. The book was published in the magazine Le Siecle, and it made the author's reputation. Le Coq appeared in several other novels between the years 1866 and 1869, but when Sherlock Holmes appeared the detective's fame subsequently declined. Holmes considered him to be a 'miserable bungler' with nothing to recommend to him save his energy. (STUD)

## LENS

(L. lens, lentil, from the similarity in form) Magnifying glass. Holmes preferred the word 'lens', probably because of its more scientific connotation. The word has a scientific usage: see E. Halley (1693): Phil. Trans. Source: RESI; GOLD; THOR; SHOS; LION; BRUC; DEVI; VALL, Ch.4

## LIFE-PRESERVER

(From c.1837) A stick or bludgeon, loaded with lead at one end, intended for self-defence. Sir George Burnwell threatened Holmes with one at his house in Streatham. Cf. Arm. Reg 11,'The prisoner was given in charge to the police a life-preserver having been found upon him'; also from The Illustrated Catalogue of The Great Exhibition, p.1056: 'Life-preservers, of whale-bone and cane, covered with leather'.
Source: NOBL; GREE; BRUC

## LITHOTYPES

(Gr. lithos, stone) A stereotypic plate made from gum-shellac, sand, tar and lindseed oil or sometimes an etched stone surface (O.E.D. 1875). Holmes' monograph 'upon the influence of a trade upon the form of the hand' displayed 'lithotypes of the hands of slaters, sailors, cork-cutters, compositors, weavers and diamond-polishers'. The O.E.D. acknowledges Doyle's use of the term.
Source: SIGN, Ch.1

## LOAFER

(Sl. Orig. 1835 - U.S. but anglicized c.1850, although Dickens uses the term in his American Notes) Idler. Loafers were a common feature in the Victorian age, often to be seen collecting on street corners and outside public houses. The wall to Lauriston Gardens was adorned with a 'small knot of loafers'. The word is probably ex. Low German from land/laufer - a landloper. Source: STUD, Ch.3.; EMPT

## LURCHER

(Connected with lurk: one who lurches: a glutton) A dog with a distinct cross of greyhound, especially a cross of greyhound and collie. Toby, whom Holmes used to trace the whereabouts of Jonathan Small and his assistant Tonga, was said to be half spaniel and half lurcher. Source: SIGN

## MAGNUM OPUS

(L.) Great work. Holmes claimed to be preparing a magnum opus which was to be the last word on the subject of criminal investigation. Its projected title was: The Whole Art Of Detection. Source: GOLD; LAST

## MARTINI BULLET

An Army rifle bullet, devised by Frederic Martini (18321897). Cf. Holmes: 'I would sooner face a Martini bullet myself. Are you game for a six-mile trudge, Watson?' - SIGN. Source: SIGN, Ch.7.

## MENDICANTS

(L. mendicare, to beg). Beggars. Holmes investigated the affair of the 'Amateur Mendicants'.    Neville St. Clair of Lee also  posed as a mendicant, adopting an ingenious disguise. Begging to a professional level like St Clair's was not unheard of in Victorian times. Indeed, shamming illness and blindness was a common trick among London's beggars. Hans Gross in his *Criminal Investigation*, cites the case of a beggar who successfully faked blindness:

'If the rogue is at liberty, he often assumes infirmities for the purpose. of begging ; blindness, deafness, paralysis, skin eruptions, and other disabilities assumed by beggars are so well-known, that they require but a passing reference. It is a common trick, too, for beggars to insinuate themselves into houses with stories of children sick at home, always taking care to add that the illness is small-pox, diphtheria, or some other contagious malady, so that to get rid of them quickly people give them alms. Blindness may be simulated in many ways, some of the crudest description. Dr. Litton Forbes (see Strand Magazine, March, 1906) mention an ingenious device. He met a man in Paris who asked for charity on the score of blindness. The writer proceeds ; ' The man attracted attention. He walked quickly and with an air of confidence He looked fixedly at me, and his eyes seemed to give expression to his thoughts. There was no uncertainty in his gaze, no shifty movements no drooping or quivering of the lids. His story told of blindness from deep-seated inflammation in both eyes, which the doctors had pronounced incurable. He had at command a rich vocabulary of technical terms, some of which he misplaced absurdly. On closer looking into, the eyes did indeed present a curious appearance. In each the pupil had almost disappeared. The iris or coloured portion had absorbed the central black spot. The pupils had become mere pinholes, but what remained of them was bright and well-defined. A glance was enough for anyone familiar with eye affections. The man was an imposter. He had instilled a drug, eserine, the active principle of the Calabar bean, into each eye This had contracted the pupils temporarily, without any permanent injury, but the appearance produced was well calculated to lend weight to his other statements.'

The order of mendicant friars was famous in medieval England. Source: FIVE; ILLU.

MICROSCOPE

Holmes considered that microscopic examination of stains in

order to identify blood corpuscles was clumsy and uncertain (STUD) and he solved the St Pancras case with the aid of his microscope. Holmes also said that Scotland Yard had begun to recognise its important is in the detection of crime (SHOS). According to Watson, grit in a sensitive instrument or a crack in one of his high-powered lenses would not be more disturbing to Holmes than a strong emotion within himself. (SCAN)

## MITRAL VALVE

(Gr. mitra, fillet) The valve in the heart which prevents blood in the left ventricle from returning to the left auricle. Thaddeus Sholto had 'grave doubts' as to his 'mitral valve' and asked Watson to examine him. Source: SIGN, Ch.4

## MONOGRAPH

A short work on a single (usually specialised) subject. Holmes claimed to have been 'guilty' of several of these. (See Appendix). Originally the word applied to a separate treatise in Natural History, e.g. on a single species, a genus or larger group of plants, animals or minerals. By 1880 the Athenaeum has (12 June, 762): 'Monographs on Poe, Hawthorne, etc.'
Source: THOR; DANC; SIGN; BRUC; HOUN, Ch.2

## MONOMANIA

An obsession of the mind by one idea or interest (from the French: monomanie). The concept of monomania was popular among certain French alienists at the turn of the century. Victor Hatherley imagined that Colonel Stark's female companion might have been a monomania. See ALIENIST.

# The Criminological Sherlock Holmes

Source: ENGR; CHAS

## MORPHINE

Holmes took morphine and cocaine by injection. (SIGN).
Whatever the philosophical or literary reasons Holmes may have
had for his initial indulgence in morphine, we should bear in
mind that the alkaloids of opium were not regarded as being as
dangerous as we know them to be today. Nevertheless, in the
1880's, when Holmes was a user, more than half the deaths by
poisons in England and Wales were due to opium and its
preparations.
Laudanum  was the commonest preparation; also a mixture
known as Godfrey's cordial which was given as a sleeping
draught to infants and young children.
Death by morphine was far less common. (a salt of morphine was
once administered to complete the work prepared by doses of
tartar emetic.) It was available to Holmes either as a white
powder or as crystals, coloured by resin. In terms of
pharmacology it was a fairly well established alkaloid by the time
Holmes began his career at Baker Street, having been discovered
by Frederich Wilhelm Serturner in 1803.
The success story of morphine was that Serturner
had isolated a pure alkaloid whose effects were predictable.
Opium itself contains many active principles beside morphine:
narcotine, thebaine, codeine, papaverine and cryptopine among
others. But morphine proved to be the most important.
Its actions on the body are many but its most important feature
comes from its direct effect on the central nervous system. If I am
correct in my assumption that Holmes suffered either from an
incurable illness or some painful physiological disorder,  then
morphine would have provided him with a blissful release from
pain. So marked is this relief that a hypodermic injection can
obliterate all sensation of pain within minutes of the morphine

entering the bloodstream. It is also, curiously, a spinal stimulant. This effect makes the user both drowsy, free from worry but also relaxed and remarkably alert. Doubt and inhibition soon fade. Its ultimate effect is to induce a deep and dreamless sleep (hence the origin of its name - after the God of Sleep, Morpheus.)

The physiological reasons for Holmes' use of morphine must also by now be apparent to the reader. It offered him instant relief so that he could concentrate his intellectual resources on the task of inductive reasoning. He was able to remain absolutely clear-headed and alert whilst under its influence. Solved too was the age-old problem of his insomnia. And his intravenous use of morphine means instant results anywhere, any time.

There are, of course, disadvantages to the drug, as Watson was only too aware. It decreases the user's respiration, provides him with pinpoint pupils and has several other unpleasant effects. Also it is highly addictive.

The evidence for Holmes' continued addiction to morphine is easy to find. Watson first suspects that his companion is taking drugs in STUD (the year of their meeting), and his suspicions are then confirmed by Holmes' own confession in SIGN. Reference is again made to the matter in SCAN, FIVE and again in CREE. In a much later case (DEVI) indirect reference is made to the problem when we learn that Holmes had been ordered to take a holiday.

A pattern of breakdowns and disruptions of Holmes' career soon becomes apparent. And when we take into account both the so-called "missing years" (did he really travel to Europe and the East or was he in a sanatorium in Switzerland ?) and his early retirement to a Sussex bee-farm the picture emerges is of a man in the grip of an indomitable addiction.

MULLER

When Holmes spoke of the "notorious Muller" in the

chemistry lab at Barts to Watson and Stamford, he was recalling a much earlier railway murder. Franz Muller was a 25 year old German tailor who, on the 9th of July 1864, murdered Thomas Briggs, a bank clerk, for his gold watch. A silk hat, found in the carriage, did not belong to Briggs and Holmesian detective work revealed the hat had been exchanged for a new one in a Cheapside shop where the jeweller identified the customer. The hat brought forward a man who recognised the owner as Muller. The murder on the 2.10 from London Bridge seventeen years later was an example of the slowness and ineptitude of the 'official police force'. At Preston Park Station, on the Brighton line, a blood-drenched young man called Arthur Lefroy staggered onto the platform from a first-class compartment.

The victim, a Mr. Gold, was later discovered lying near the entrance to Balcombe tunnel. He had been shot in the back of the neck and had been attacked by a knife. As Lefroy related a fantastic story about two men who had attacked him and then disappeared from the carriage, the ticket collector noticed a watch chain hanging from his shoe. Lefroy claimed it belonged to him. Surprisingly, Lefroy impressed the railway police with his story. However, they insisted he be escorted home to Croydon. The detective sergeant who accompanied him was one George Holmes, a man with 11 years' experience with the Metropolitan force who was seconded to the railway.

When Lefroy returned to Cathcart Road, Croydon, in the company of Holmes, he was asked to make a statement about the number on the back of the watch. Lefroy got it wrong. Neither did he know its make. The detective's suspicions, incredibly, were not aroused in the slightest. When he returned to Wallington station and discovered that the watch in Lefroy's possession actually belonged to the victim, Holmes sprinted back to Cathcart Road only to find that the bird had flown. Lefroy was eventually traced through a telegram which he sent to his employer, asking for wages. Intriguingly, it was a Mr. Doyle, a neighbour of

Lefroy's who delivered the fateful telegram into the hands of the police.
The Lefroy case was one of the worst examples of incompetence by the Yard and there were others, notably the Ripper case.

## MULTIPLEX KNIVES

(L. multiplex-plicare, to fold) A knife with several blades. Holmes claimed that the killer of Lord Brackenstall had one in his possession. Source: ABBE

## NARK

(Si. Romany nak, nose) An informer: a police spy, as copper's nark: one who curries favour, a pick-thank. Source: ILLU

## NERVOUS LESIONS

(Fr. lesion - L. laesio-onis-laedere, laesum, to hurt) Damage to the brain or central nervous system caused by disease or injury. Percy Trevelyan had written a monograph on the subject and Watson had read it. Source: RESI

## NITRATE OF AMYL

(From nitre: sodium carbonate and amyl, an alcohol radical C5 - H11) Usually nitrite of amyl. A solution used for the treatment of certain nervous disorders. Percy Trevelyan suggested the medicine as a cure for his supposed Russian patient's catalepsy.
( RESI) In RESI, Dr Trevelyan relates how he attempted to treat his patient  for the rare condition known as catalepsy. He recommends nitrate of amyl since he had "obtained good results in such cases by the inhalation (of the drug.)" This was used by some Victorian doctors as an alternative to smelling salts. Amyl

nitrate is a clear yellow liquid with a characteristic odour. The modern method is to administer the drug by inhalation from glass capsules but in the last century it was supplied from a bottle. Dr Trevelyan used amyl as a muscle relaxant. It can also be employed for its relaxant action in the relief of biliary colic and spasmodic asthma.

OCCIPITAL BONE

(L. occiput: ob - over against; caput - head) The bone that forms the back of the skull. James McCarthy 's father's occipital bone was shattered (BOSC). Source: BOSC

OPIUM

(See also MORPHINE.) A drug derived from the dried juice of poppies. In Victorian times it was patented in remedies such as laudanum, morphine and paregoric. It was Britain's commercial interests which led to the Chinese Opium Wars and which later led to a powerful lobby among M.P's to ban the import of opium into Britain. Opium was widely used in several medicinal preparations during the 19th Century, including paregoric (q.v.), laudanum (q.v.) and   morphine (q.v.). Holmes himself injected himself with the latter (SIGN). The tragedy of opium and morphine addiction among 19th Century users (including Coleridge and De Quincey) was that they simply did not appreciate its addictive qualities. Dr Alexander Wood, the American who perfected the hypodermic syringe in 1853, lost his own wife when she died from an overdose of morphine. Yet morphine was widely used as an anaesthetic. Watson regarded Holmes as being 'well-up in opium and other poisons (STUD, Ch.1); Isa Whitney became addicted to opium smoking; the sepoy mutineers were drunk with opium (SIGN); Ned Hunter was drugged by opium (SILV) whilst Ian Murdoch cried out for it after his attack by Cyanea Capillata. (LION). In TWIS Watson visits an opium den and finds Holmes there. See MORPHINE.

## PALMER, WILLIAM

"When a doctor does go wrong he is the first of criminals. Palmer and Pritchard were among the heads of their profession" — Holmes, SPEC.

Palmer's trial took place in 1856. He qualified at St. Barts in 1846 and began practice in Rugeley, Staffordshire. He married, had an affair with his servant and frequently got into debt. He resolved then to poison his mother-in-law so that her estate would pass to his wife and eventually to him. Palmer's four children died, then his wife and brother (after they had been insured for very large sums). Palmer was a compulsive gambler and in 1855 attended Shrewsbury Races with a friend, John Cook. Cook won large sums while Palmer lost. Having collected Cook's winnings for him, Palmer then poisoned his companion. Unfortunately for Palmer, the autopsy showed evidence of antimony. Palmer was subsequently arrested and hanged in 1856.

## PAREGORIC

(L. paregoricus) Paregoric elixir. A solution of opium, benzoic acid, camphor and oil of anise in alcohol, used as a pain killer. Holmes recommends the use of a paregoric (somewhat unkindly) as a cure for the maid Susan's wheezing. Cf. British Pharmacoepia, Nov. 1888: 'any medicine that assuages pain, an anodyne'. Source: 3GAB

## PARIETAL BONE

(L. parietalis, paries, parietis, a wall) One of two bones situated at

the side and back of the skull. James McCarthy's father had the posterior third of the left parietal bone shattered (BOSC). Dr Mortimer (HOUN) asked Holmes if he would have any objection to his running his finger along his (Holmes') parietal fissure.
Source: BOSC; HOUN, Ch.1

## PATHOLOGY

The study and diagnosis of disease. Pathology addresses four components of disease, cause, mechanisms of development, structural alteration of cells and the consequences of changes. In SIGN, Watson plunged into the latest treatise on the subject, whilst in CREE Holmes spoke about Professor Presbury 'with the air of a pathologist who presents a rare specimen.'

## PEACE, CHARLES

"My old friend Charlie Peace was a violin virtuoso." - Holmes, ILLU.
Born 1832, Peace was perhaps Victorian England's most elusive burglar. Agile, strong and described as a "monkey of a man", he was an expert in disguise and had a flair for theatricals and music. (The violin case often contained his burgling tools!) Whilst in Manchester, Peace murdered his neighbour, Dyson, after pestering his wife and was also responsible for the shooting of PC Nicholas Cook. Three Irishmen were mistakenly convicted of this later crime. Peace, now with a reward on his head, moved to London. While burgling a house in Blackheath on 10 October 1878, he was arrested by PC Edward Robinson, after a struggle, and tried for attempted murder in November. Sentenced to life imprisonment, he made a daring escape attempt by jumping out of a train bound for Sheffield but was immediately recaptured. Whilst awaiting execution for Cook's murder he made a full confession of his previous crimes. Arthur Griffiths' interview with

Peace in his Mysteries of Police and Crime reveals a ruthless but colourful character with an ingenious turn of mind. How and when Holmes met Peace is open to speculation.

## PENAL SERVITUDE

(L. poenalis, poena: Gr. poine, punishment) A type of imprisonment. The minimum allowable sentence was three years which was reducible by a quarter for good behaviour. Penal servitude usually involved hard labour in convict gangs. The term is derived from the original notion which involved the confiscation of the criminal's property and his reduction of status to that of a slave. Holmes suggested that the thief who appropriated the blue carbuncle would get 'seven years' penal servitude. Source: BLUE; STOC; DANC

## PINFIRE REVOLVER

A revolver fitted with a pin enabling the hammer to strike the powder in the cartridge. A revolver of this type was found in Wisteria Lodge. Source: WIST

## PINNA

(L. pinna, a feather, dim. pinnuta) The broad part of the upper, external ear. Holmes uses the term in referring to Sarah Cushing's amputated ear. Source: CARD

## PIPETTE

(Fr, dim. of pipe, pipe) A tube for transferring and measuring fluids and gases. Holmes used one at his chemical corner in Baker Street. Source: STUD, Ch.1; NAVA

## PLASTER OF PARIS

A quick setting plaster which is invaluable for filling cavities where a footprint has been detected. Holmes' monograph on the tracing the footsteps including remarks on the uses of plaster of Paris as a preserver of impresses. In Hans Gross' monumental book, Criminal Investigation, there is a detailed account of the process which no doubt, Holmes himself used:

'As to the dilution of the plaster of paris there is but one thing to remember. If the water be poured upon the powdered plaster it forms into a mass of pasty clots which will not penetrate into all the intricacies of the footprint.
These clots would require to be broken up, an operation requiring so much time that the plaster would commence to set before it was completed. To remedy this inconvenience a vase should be used, half filled with water, into which spoonfuls of the powdered plaster are poured, or, better still, passed through a sieve, so that the surface of the water is equally and several
times powdered over. This is continued until a little eminence forms just rising above the level of the water. At this stage no more plaster is poured in, and the mixture of water and plaster is rapidly stirred.
The result is, a homogeneous soup without lumps or clots, which is poured on to the footprint. The operation must be performed rapidly in order that the plaster may not harden. But too great quickness must be avoided, or the layers of the soup in forming upon one another would produce air bubbles, and the corresponding spot upon the footprint would remain empty. The best method is for one person to pour the plaster of paris slowly into the footprint while another spreads it carefully with
a spoon, as it falls without touching the footprint, and thus assisting it to penetrate into all the parts.
During this operation, at the moment when the ground is covered

with a bed of plaster of about one centimetre's thickness, small pieces of prepared wood should be placed, by a third person if possible, upon the plaster, after which the remainder is poured out. If the footprint be very deep, we may when these sticks have been covered with about one centimetre of plaster, further superimpose yet more pieces of stick. These pieces of wood are intended to form a skeleton inside the plaster cast and thus to give it more solidity. The plaster may be also stiffened in another way. Besides the pieces of wood, twisted string may be placed, giving both solidity and stiffness. It should be remembered that the wood, as also the string, should be soaked beforehand in water, so as to be thoroughly wet through. Without this precaution the wood and the string would absorb water from the plaster of paris, swell, and cause the whole to split. It is also advisable, in this case, to allow certain of these ribbons to project, thus enabling the mould to be seized and lifted up, when the right moment has come.

As regards the period of the operation, it will be found that good plaster thickens in a few minutes and becomes fairly set after about ten minutes. The mould may then be lifted up. The fact that good plaster sets so quickly and develops a certain quantity of heat has the further advantage of not hindering the work even during a hard frost. Only when the cold is extremely severe will it be advisable to light a small fire on the side whence comes the wind, in order to raise the temperature during the time necessary for the plaster to set. When the cast has been lifted it must be examined to see how far it corresponds with the footprint, and in the report the faults, omissions, etc., which have been produced will be most minutely noted down. Little pieces of earth, etc., sticking to the  cast may be removed as explained above by means of a wetted brush.'

# The Criminological Sherlock Holmes

## POISONS

"POISON - Any substance which, when introduced into or
absorbed by a living organism, destroys life or injures health." -
The Shorter Oxford Dictionary
"I dabble with poisons a good deal." - Sherlock Holmes, STUD.


Holmes was 'well up' in his knowledge of poisons generally
according to Watson and poisons featured in a number of his
cases, including STUD, DEVI, GREE, SIGN,  SILV, LADY,
RETI, SPEC GOLD, CREE,DYIN, and SUSS. Types of poison
used comprised curare, snake venom, coal gas, strychnine,
opium, and chloroform (see entries). Holmes also defined himself
as a 'self poisoner' by cocaine and tobacco.
The last two decades of the nineteenth century were crucial to the
scientist and criminal investigator alike regarding poisons. They
were pioneering years both in Europe and America. Before the
80's the weight of evidence which went to condemn a murderer to
the gallows often depended upon eye witness reports. By the turn
of the century, the whole modus operandus of the criminologist
was starting to transform the Surete and Scotland Yard.
These were the virgin years, during which a number of isolated
pioneers dominated the literature of the scientific journals.
Toxicology, the study of poisons, had remained largely
unchanged since the era of Mathieu Orfila, the "father of
toxicology", who, in the 1840's, had played such a vital part in the
Lafarge case.
There was, even in the later years of the nineteenth century, a
great deal of mystery and confusion surrounding the subject of
poisons, so much so that when Dr William Guy published his
"Principles of Forensic Medicine" (1861), he had to declare
that "the term poison does not admit of strict definition". This is
true even now, for the effect of a poison depends purely on its
dosage and what will kill one man may have even beneficial

effects upon another.

The pioneering work carried out by Orfila (particularly in the field of arsenic examination) was continued by one of his pupils, Sir Robert Christison (1797-1882), who was appointed to the chair of forensic medicine in Edinburgh. In 1829 he published his seminal "Treatise On Poisons", which was to remain for many years the most authoritative English work on the subject.

Christison's breakthrough was in establishing that, despite the problem of definition, poisons all had one thing in common: they were all substances which caused chemical and psychological changes in the body, sometimes resulting in tissue damage and malfunction of the nervous system.

He was also able to classify poisons into four main categories: a) poisons which cause interruption to the oxygen carrying capacity of the blood ( cyanide, carbon monoxide), b) poisons which cause corrosive damage (acids, alkalis), c) systemic poisons, which are absorbed through the skin or intestinal tract and which cause damage to the main organs (arsenic, antimony) This category includes the vegetable alkaloids (strychnine, morphine, etc.) which affect the central nervous system and its operation, d) a further category of poisons which leave no trace of entry but which cause destruction after absorption (Ricin, arsine, etc.)

By the time that Sherlock Holmes had abandoned a rural existence for the investigation of crime at St Barts Hospital, advances in toxicology in England had been piecemeal and far from comprehensive. In fact the latter part of the nineteenth century saw the appearance of many remarkable names in the field of scientific and medical examination. Many of these names the aspiring criminologist like Holmes would have found familiar to his ears.

There was Joseph Lister, whose development of antiseptics was revolutionising the work of the surgeon both in Edinburgh and London. He had come to London in 1877, taking with him four of his faithful assistants to help him in his crusade. All over the world, except in London, surgeons were now adopting his new ideas. Asepsis is now used in hospitals throughout the world, but in those far off days of the '70's and '80's the operating theatre was often far from spotless and the death rate from post-operative infection was far too high.

As the Listerian revolution spread, Joseph Lister gained universal acknowledgement as the leading surgeon of his age, so much so that by 1883, when he was 56, Queen Victoria awarded him a baronetcy.

Another name familiar to the lean-faced figure bent over the retort stand in that dingy chemical laboratory at Bart's was that of Louis Pasteur.

In many respects, advances in medicine moved at a greater pace than in the somewhat more conservative field of the forensic sciences. In Britain investigatory work was the province of the coroner rather than the police surgeon, and it was not until Professor Hans Gross published his System der Kriminalistik (first published in English in 1906) that the English police began to accept a more scientific approach to crime investigation.

Again, it was Europe rather than Europe that led the field of contact trace examination with the work of Edmond Locard (1910). And it was the University of Lausanne in Switzerland rather than an English university which offered the first course in criminalistics for students (1902).

Young Stamford, who acted as a dresser under Watson whilst at Darts, makes an illuminating comment about Holmes:

"Holmes is a little too scientific for my tastes (he observes) - it approaches to cold-bloodedness. I could imagine his giving a friend a little pinch of the latest vegetable alkaloid, not out of malevolence, you understand, but simply out of a spirit of enquiry in order to have an accurate idea of its effects. To do him justice, I think that he would take it himself with the same readiness. He appears to have a passion for definite and exact knowledge." (STUD)

Elsewhere, whilst citing Holmes' limits, friend Watson observes that his companion is "well up in belladonna, opium, and poisons generally".

The suggestion in both these passages is that Holmes had made and was making a particular study of the alkaloids. This is not really surprising since Victorian England was littered with the victims of alkaloidal poisons. The age of the manufactured, synthetic poisons (the barbiturates, for example) was yet to arrive.

To the Victorian gentleman the most unobtrusive method by which to dispose of his spouse or business rivals was to obtain one of the readily available mixtures, which in that era could be bought over the shop counter. Some were prepared for household, some for veterinary and some for garden use: weed-killer, rat poison, etc.

There were a great number of proprietary medicines which also held poisonous ingredients and which could be obtained without trouble: Fowler's solution (arsenic), Easton's syrup (strychnine) and laudanum ( a solution of morphine). Attempts to regulate these poisons did not begin until the Arsenic Act of 1851, but even then it was only required that the purchaser of the poison should be known by the seller.

It was not until 1868 that the range of controlled poisons was broadened and pharmacists were compelled to keep a note of their sales. Even then it was possible for the enterprising poisoner to obtain his or her poisons by devious methods.

Britain had to wait until 1933 (Pharmacy and Poisons Act) for the first truly comprehensive system which governed not only the sale but also the labelling, storage and transportation of drugs.

In studying the alkaloidal poisons, Holmes chose to investigate the oldest group of drugs known to man. However, since the last century the crude vegetable drugs like strychnine, to which this variety belongs, has declined (except for digitalis which is still used for the treatment of heart conditions) and the synthetic drugs have come to the fore.

The word "alkaloid" refers to the active ingredient of a drug or poison. They are basic substances that can combine with acids to form salts ( e.g. morphine tartrate, atropine sulphate).

Their composition is constant and their action consistent.

In the '80's toxicology was a minor branch of pharmacology, which itself was a development of the study of the materia medica (some chairs of pharmacology are still called chairs of materia medica - especially in Edinburgh and Glasgow).

The student was expected to have a good general grounding in botany ( Watson refers to Holmes' knowledge of botany as "variable" - STUD), so that he could check medicines and their preparation.

In the second half of of the 19th Century there was a developing interest in the efficiency and application of the plant preparations and there were a number of experiments carried out by researchers, often upon themselves. The results of these often hazardous experiments were published regularly in the British Medical Journal. (Conan Doyle was known to have used himself as a guinea pig.)

The great inquisition into both the useful and harmful plant preparations was well advanced by the 1870's and Holmes was evidently part of this tide of growing enthusiasm.

The era of innovation coincided with the manufacture of substances produced in the chemical laboratory. In Germany in 1862 Liebig produced Choral hydrate, a sleep-producing drug. This was followed by the production of salicylic acid, a drug which lowered body temperature in cases of fever (Buss, 1875) and in 1886 Cahn and Hepp described a similar action for acetanilide. By the turn of the century (1899) Dreser had synthesised the wonder drug aspirin and the once addictive cocaine, pioneered by Dr Freud of Vienna, had been safely converted into procaine (1905).

With the new drugs came new poisons and the study

of toxicology grew more complex. For Holmes, the vegetable-derived substances were invariably used upon the victims he encountered. Hence, the long hours spent in the old chemistry lab at Barts provided him with the ground work necessary for a criminologist of his stature and expertise. As Stamford put it to Watson: "he is a first-class chemist... his studies are very desultory and eccentric, but has amassed a lot of out-of-the-way knowledge which would astonish his professors" - STUD.


## POLE-AXED

Struck down with a pole-axe (a butcher's axe with a hammer-faced back).
Source: MISS; REDC

## PRITCHARD, EDWARD

A Glasgow physician who poisoned his wife and mother-in-law with aconite, Pritchard was an egotist of the first order, gave travel lectures about places he had never even visited, became a Freemason and handed out signed photographs of himself. His motive for murder appears to have been a promise he made to a 15 year old servant girl whom he made pregnant, then aborted. Pritchard would never have been caught save for an anonymous letter sent to the Procurator-Fiscal. He was hanged in July 1865. Holmes' remarks regarding the errant doctor were indeed apt. The Stoke Moran affair (SPEC) took place in April 1883. Only a year before Dr George Henry Lamson had poisoned his 18 year old brother-in-law with a little known vegetable poison, aconitine, contained in a capsule of sugar. He was executed in April 1882.

## PRUSSIC ACID

Hydrocyanic acid, a colourless, deadly liquid with a distinctive almond smell. So-called because it was first obtained from Prussian blue, ferric ferrocyanide, a colour pigment, discovered in Berlin. Mrs Merrilow had considered taking prussic acid.
Source: VEIL

## RADIX PEDIS DIABOLI

(L.) Devil's root foot. A powerful hallucinogenic drug that killed Brenda and Mortimer Tregennis and Brenda's two brothers. The drug, as described above, cannot be found in the Western Pharmacoepiae. According to Dr Sterndale it was virtually unknown among Western toxicologists. The root is shaped like a foot, half human, half-goat-like; hence the fanciful name given by a botanical missionary.
Source: DEVI. See DEVIL'S FOOT ROOT.

## RATCLIFFE HIGHWAY MURDER

Referred to in the newspaper report in STUD. Ratcliff Highway is a road in the London borough of Stepney, subsequently renamed St. George's Street. Holmes, it will be recalled, sent "a couple of messages" to "Sumner, shipping Agent" in BLAC. A number of murders took place here in the early 19th century. On December 7, 1811, a family known as the Marrs were found brutally murdered in their East End shop. In less than a fortnight another massacre occurred. This time the victims were the landlord and his wife in a pub in Gravel Lane. Four days later an Irish sailor was arrested on suspicion of the murders. His name was Williams. At first, the evidence was hardly convincing. Fresh evidence, collected from witnesses who knew the publican, was only circumstantial (for instance, a laundress, who washed

William's linen, stated he had given her a shirt to wash which was torn and bloodstained.) While the inquiry was still in progress, Williams hanged himself in his cell at Coldbath Fields prison. Although Williams' and Marrs' pasts were connected, no real motive for the murders of the victims was satisfactorily established.

## RECTIFIED SPIRITS

(Fr. rectifier: L.L. rectificare, to make) Purified or distilled alcohol. Referring to a severed ear, Holmes observed that a medical mind would have preserved the trophy in 'carbolic' or 'rectified spirits'. Source: CARD

## RED REPUBLICAN

(L. respublica, commonwealth) A revolutionary or radical advocate of .republicanism, i.e. that form of government which rejects monarchy and in which supreme power is vested in the people and their elected representatives. Morse Hudson commented that his bust of Napoleon may have been destroyed by red republicans. Source: SIXN

## REMINGTON

A type of American typewriter manufactured by the gun making firm  E Remmington & Sons of New York .Laura Lyons had such a typewriter. (HOUN)

## REVERSION

(L. reversare, to turn round)  A return to an ancestral type;  a term used in the discussion of heredity. See ATAVISM.
Source: HOUN, Ch.1

## RICOLETTI

"Here's the record of... Ricoletti of the club-foot, and his abominable wife." — MUSG

Speculation has been varied about his case. D.A.Redmond (SHJ Vol. 12 No. 1) inclines to the view that "Ricoletti" was a synonym of "Miletti the Jemmy", a nickname conferred on a member of the famous Camorra, the Neapolitan underworld.

## RIGOR MORTIS

(L. rigor-rigere, to be stiff) Stiffening of the body after death, by the muscles. In SIGN Holmes observed that Bartholomew Sholto's muscular contraction was more pronounced than that usually attributable to rigor mortis.
Source: SIGN

## RISUS SARDONICUS

A sardonic grin, caused by the drawing back of the corners of the mouth by an involuntary spasm of the muscles. The condition is often caused by tetanus. In SIGN, Bartholomew Sholto displayed this feature after his death from some 'curare-like substance'.
Source: SIGN, Ch.6

## ST BARTS

It was in the chemical laboratory at St Barts where the first meeting between Holmes and Watson took place.
We also learn from Watson's narrative in STUD: 1) that Holmes dabbles a great deal in poisons and b) that he carried out a bizarre experiment in the dissecting rooms, "beating the subjects with a

stick to verify how far bruises may be produced after death."
From this we can only conclude that he must have had a free run
of the 'labs' and unsupervised access to chemical and anatomical
equipment there.

In 1881 Bart's was a thriving centre for much that was new in
medical knowledge at the time. Until 1865 the dissecting rooms
had been used every summer for chemistry classes but in that
year it was decided to provide a chemical classroom to
accommodate 130 students. In 1870 a new chemical lab was built
with a lecture theatre for 100 persons and a preparation room. In
1876 the Medical School was entirely rebuilt, paid for by the
Charity Commissioners. The new anatomical theatre held 300
students (it was later destroyed by a bomb in 1940). The
dissecting room, where Holmes spent his time beating corpses,
was enlarged to twice its original size and a gallery added to it
which housed the Anatomical Museums. This unique collection
would have afforded particular interest to Holmes the
criminologist, for amongst its exhibits was the skull of John
Bellingham who in 1812 was executed for the murder of the
Right Hon. Spencer Perceval, Prime Minister — a unique case in
the annals of British crime.

The new buildings were completed in the very year that Dr.
Watson struck up an acquaintanceship with his eccentric fellow
lodger. At that time the Medical School provided the best
accommodation in the country to its students.

If times were hard and the expenses high for the students in the
medical school, so equally did the hospital struggle against
hardships. Nurses worked an incredible 15 hour day. Patients
were usually chloroformed for serious operations and the success
rate was high. But by today's standards, the operating theatres
suffered somewhat primitive conditions. One nurse described
conditions in pre-anaesthetic days in the following terms (one
must remember that things had improved somewhat by Holmes'

day):

'It still contained the table on which formerly patients were strapped for the operation.... The cupboards were antiquated; there was one containing sand, and, when the surgeon felt the floor getting sticky, he called for this and the nurse took a shovelful from the cupboard, and spread it on the floor.'

Attempting to throw some light on the elusive Mr. Holmes' attendance (or non-attendance) of lectures at the time, A.N. Griffith attempts to demonstrate Holmes' connection with Norman Moore, who was later to become something of a celebrity in British Medicine. According to Mr. Griffith: 'Augustus Mattiessen was the lecturer in chemistry at Barts from 1870 onwards. Sir Norman Moore recalls that he had two private pupils; one was Moore himself, the other he does not mention.... He had been in Strasbourg during the Franco-Prussian war... when a shell passed through his house; Mattiessen was interested in opium and together they investigated its alkaloids....'

The stranger's involvement in the Franco-Prussian War, Mr. Griffith advises us, would account for Holmes' absence from Britain during the Adventure of The Noble Bachelor and also his smattering of German.
Mr. Griffith's theory is an interesting one. Unfortunately, his information is incorrect since Mattiessen ceased lecturing in chemistry in 1870. However, a connection between the mysterious stranger and Moore himself is not an unlikely assumption. At the time of Holmes' attendance, the lecturer in chemistry was W.J. Russell (another Russell, not the author of those sea stories Watson adored!) A popular man with the students, he had to provide his own apparatus and pay for his own private lab at Bart's. Holmesians may be intrigued to know that in 1880 Russell was appointed a member of a committee set up to

investigate the chemical properties of fog! His other work included the investigation of ancient Egyptian pigments and colouring in flowers.

Moore himself was at school with Russell before going to Owen's College, Manchester. During Holmes' attendance, he became lecturer on comparative anatomy, a field of passionate interest to the young detective. Is it not conceivable that Holmes and Moore were on exceedingly good terms with each other and that a special arrangement was subsequently made for the apprentice criminologist?

The lecturer in pathological anatomy, at the time was John Wickham Legg (1878-87) whilst forensic medicine lay mainly in the hands of Reginald Southey. It was George Burrows, the prototype Victorian consulting physician, who largely promoted forensic medicine.

As the authors of *The Royal Hospital of St. Barts* point out (Medvei and Thornton), "the content of the subject was all those questions relating to the death or injury of individuals, whether arising from violence, accidents, or any other sudden cause." Legg himself was an expert on haemophilia, the disease which plagued Queen Victoria's offspring. He was also the author of a monograph entitled Some Account of Cardiac Aneurysms. This appeared some three years after the Jefferson Hope affair had been satisfactorily concluded.

Hope himself died from an aortic aneurysm, a localized enlargement of an artery due to pressure of blood acting on a weak part. (Holmes' interest in cardiac arrest was further stimulated, it will be remembered, in his investigation of the death of Sir Charles Baskerville.) Southey contributed a monograph on The Nature and Affinites of Tubercle, a study which marked the 'death throes of the concept of the spontaneous origins of infections within the tissues and organs of the human body.'

The thorough-going working knowledge of poisons which

# The Criminological Sherlock Holmes

Holmes acquired must surely have been nurtured at this period in his career. One of his mentors must certainly have been Thomas Lauder Brunton, a Scotsman who studied medicine at Edinburgh in 1866. He came to the Royal Infirmary later than Holmes' residence, although as early as 1868, he had produced an authoritative monograph on the possible danger of over-use of the drug digitalis. It was, of course, a "digitalis-like substance" which accounted for the death of Bartholomew Sholto and it was more than likely that Watson, himself a Bart's man, had read Brunton's work. In 1885 he published the Textbook of pharmacology and therapeutics, a work which through the subsequent 90's was to stand as the principal work upon the subject. A copy of this magnum opus must have adorned a bookshelf in the rooms of 221b. (Curiously, Brunton was the name of the unfortunate butler in MUSG. Is this an echo?)

Finally, a curiosity volume of immense interest to Holmes, the 'dabbler in poisons,' must surely have been George Roupell's Illustrations of the effects of poisons which contained 'eight large coloured lithographs' showing the effects of various poisons on dogs. Roupell injected arsenic and tartar emetic into the veins of a number of dogs. Holmes, you will recall, was not averse to conducting a similar experiment in STUD when he killed Mrs. Hudson's terrier without a qualm.

As a prime Sherlock Holmes location, St Barts is not generally open to the public since it is a working medical facility. Holmesian scholars have identified a room where the legendary meeting first took place and several years ago a commemorative plaque was installed by the Sherlock Holmes Society of London. However, this has now been moved into the hospital's Museum. Visitors can visit the Museum to see the plaque from Tuesday to Friday from 10 AM to 4 PM except on bank holidays and the museum itself shows a variety of medical relics some of which would have been used during the period of Dr Watson's practice.

## SCOTLAND YARD

Shortly before departing for the Brixton Road, Holmes remarks to Watson that 'Gregson is the smartest of the Scotland Yarders... he and Lestrade are the pick of a bad lot.'

Holmes' remarks are telling. The police had never been popular with the general public and were frequently satirised in the pages of Punch. Only four years before Holmes investigated the Brixton Road murder, London had been shocked by the trial of Scotland Yard detectives.

The Yard's first commissioner, Sir Edmund Henderson, was allowed to increase the Detective Department of the Metropolitan Police to 207. 180 of these men were to be plain clothes policemen and the other 27 were to work from headquarters. Gregson and Lestrade came from that small elite whose record of honesty and experience had been sullied.

The exposee came after the trials at the Old Bailey of a gang of swindlers. Harry Benson and Frederick Kurt had been charged with falsely obtaining £10,000 from a wealthy French woman, Madame de Goncourt. The trick was to obtain bets from France by posing as an English gentleman who had inside knowledge on the favourites in certain races. When the cheques arrived they were quickly cashed and the customers of 'Mr. Montgomery', the English gentleman, heard no more.

Through the efforts of Inspector Williamson, Benson and Kurt were arrested. The scandal erupted when other members of the gang began to make statements about leading Scotland Yard detectives who were working as accomplices in the operation. Four of these men, Chief Inspectors Druscovitch (a Pole), Palmer, Clarke and Meiklejohn were arrested and charged. Only Clarke was found not guilty at the conclusion of the three weeks' trial. The others were sentenced to two year's hard labour.

A report of the Home Office Committee suggested an overhaul of the Detective Department and under Howard Vincent, an enterprising barrister, sweeping reforms were commenced along the lines of the French Surete. The Department was centralised along with its records and was thereafter known as the CID (Criminal Investigation Department).

It is not difficult, therefore, to see why Holmes had such little time for the 'Scotland Yarders' as he called them. Nevertheless, later in his career, his attitude softened towards them. In 3GAB, for example, he remarks that they 'lead the world for thoroughness and method.'

At the time of STUD, the official police force had made a few advances and had acknowledged some of the techniques offered by the forensic scientist. However, the bulk of the work pursued by the CID was based heavily on a body of informers who provided inside information on the movements of the underworld. This had existed long before the formation of Peel's New Police. The Bow Street Runners, for instance, had a considerable liaison network with their 'squealers' and one of Peel's reasons for reforming the system was their excessive reliance on this system and the acceptance of bribes.

The Met. Police, conservative in their approach, and subject to a rigid heirarchy, were reluctant to adopt new methods unless they had been rigorously proven. Indeed, their inability to solve the Ripper murder has often been put down to this fact. (All but one of the Ripper's victims was removed from the scene of the crime, the bodies washed and vital clues thus destroyed.)

The field was therefore left wide open. But the consulting detective was indeed a rarity. There were of course agencies like the one in Wych Street (now the Aldwych), but their function was limited to matters of civil or domestic dispute. Most private investigators did not have the range or variety of work encountered by Holmes and many of them were employed on what could be politely termed the 'legal borderlands.'

## SCOWRERS

(sl. 17th C., 18th C.) A band of wild and boisterous men who roamed the streets, terrorising people. The Molly Maguires were so-named. The word originates from stover, scowre, to decamp or run away. The v.i. is 'to roam noisily about at night, smashing windows, waylaying and beating wayfarers, attacking the watch' (Shadwell, Prior). Source: VALL, Pt.2

## SINGLE-STICK

A heavy wooden stick approximately three feet long with a protected handle at one end. Originally designed for sabre-training, it became, in the late Victorian period, a weapon in its own right. Single-stick combat was a popular sport in Victorian gymnasiums. Holmes professed to being a 'bit of a single-stick expert'. Source: ILLU; STUD, Ch.2

## SMASHER

(sl. Imit; cf. Sw. dial. smaske, to smack) One who passes bad or counterfeit money. Source: REDH

## SNACKLED

(Sl. Cf. snabbled or snaffled: to arrest, to capture - etymology dubious. Cf. Du. snavel: **Ger.** schnabel, beak, mouth) Jefferson Hope said that he was 'neatly snackled' by Holmes. Source: STUD

## SPINAL MENINGITIS

(Gr. meninx-ingos, a membrane) An infectious disease which inflames the membranes of the spinal cord. It was supposed that

Bob Ferguson's pet spaniel was suffering from this condition.
Source: SUSS

## STAUNTON, HENRY

"There is Arthur H. Staunton, the rising young forger... and there
was Henry Staunton, whom I helped to hang.... " MISS 3
This could have been a reference to the Staunton brothers who, in
1877, were charged with the murder of Louis Staunton's 36 year
old wife. It was claimed that they, with the assistance of Patrick
Staunton's wife and Louis' mistress, had starved her to death at a
house in Penge. However, they were reprieved from the death
sentence because of the unconvincing nature of the evidence
against them. Alice Rhodes was released. The others served out
prison sentences. However, since the Stauntons did not hang, we
must assume that Henry Staunton was involved in another
murder. No doubt the Stauntons found a place in Holmes' index.

## STEVENS, BERT

"You remember that terrible murderer, Bert Stevens, who wanted
us to get him off in '87?" — NORW.

According to Michael Harrison (*The World of Sherlock Holmes*)
Bert Stevens was a cover-name for James Kenneth Stephen, tutor
to the Duke of Clarence (Prince Albert, eldest son of King
Edward VII). In 1892 Stephen died in an asylum from a mania
which lasted two and a half months. Harrison believes that
Stephen was Jack the Ripper and that Holmes, in order to avert a
scandal, was called in to investigate on behalf of the ageing
Victoria. Thus the true identity of the Ripper had to remain a
secret.

STOOL PIGEON

(orig. U.S. slang. Anglicized by 1916) A decoy: a police informer.
(Shortened form: stoolie) Used by Holmes as part of his
intelligence. Irish American slang (LAST). SOURCE: LAST

STRYCHNINE

(Gr. strychnos, nightshade)  A highly poisonous alkaloid
($C2H22N202$) obtained from flux vomica seeds. Strychnine
stimulates the vaso-nator centre and causes a contraction of the
blood vessels and an increase in blood pressure. Death results
either from asphyxia or exhaustion of the nerve centre. Enoch J.
Drebber (STUD) died of strychnine poisoning (in this author's
opinion) as did Bartholomew Sholto (SIGN).

SUBCLAVIAN (ARTERY)

(Prefix: sub - under; clavicle - collar-bone) A large artery situated
at the base of the neck. The jezail bullet which wounded Watson
at the fatal battle of Maiward "grazed" his subclavian artery.
Source: STUD, Ch.1

SUBCUTANEOUSLY

(L. sub - under; cutis - the skin) Under the skin. John Straker
nicked a horse's tendons in this manner and Holmes administered
cocaine to himself in this way. Source: SILV; SIGN

SWAG

(sl. Related to sway: prob. Scand.) Booty, plunder, e.g: 'But he'll
let us slip if we only tell him where the swag is'. By 1890 the
word implied any unlawful gains, e.g. Dickens, 1838: "'It's all

arranged about bringing off the swag is it?" asked the Jew. Sikes nodded'. (Oliver Twist) Source: MAZA; BOSC

## SWAMP ADDER

According to Holmes, an Indian swamp adder killed Julia Stoner and Dr Grimesby Roylott. There is, however, no snake known to science as a 'speckled band'. Several vipers could be considered. However, Holmes states that Roylott died 'within ten seconds' of being bitten. In fact there is no snake venom that would kill a man or woman in that time. Both types of Indian viper - the Elapidae and the Viperidae kill by haemotoxic venom which acts on the blood; but Watson does not describe the familiar symptoms of viper poisoning in his account. The identity of the swamp adder' therefore remains something of a mystery. Source: SPEC

## TAPANULI FEVER

An invented disease, probably derived from Tapanodi Bay or Subolga Bay, an inlet of the Indian Ocean on the north west coast of Sumatra. Holmes asked Watson what he knew of the disease. Source: DYIN

## TATTOOS

Holmes had made a small study of tattooo marks and had written a monograph on the subject. (See Appendix): (REDH). Jabez Wilson (REDH) had a tattoo of a fish above his right wrist which was a delicate shade of pink and which Holmes commented on as being 'quite peculiar to China.' In GLOR Trevor Senior had the initials JA tattooed in the bend of his elbow which he had tried to obscure.
According to Hans Gross in his Criminal Investigation:

'Tattooings which exist or which have existed on the bodies of living or dead persons may be very important in determining identity ; they must therefore be examined and described in detail. Let it also be stated that attention must be paid to tattooings which are no longer visible ; there is no doubt that they may disappear from view ; they fade away either through lapse of time or, if the work has been badly done or unstable colours have been used, even after a short time. They may also be made to disappear artificially by submitting them to the corrosive action of an acid, especially indigo extract (indigotin disulphonic acid), ( Deuchatel) .

'Dr. Variot  mentions a device whereby nothing but a scar is left ; the application of a paste containing salicylic acid and glycerine (for about a week's time) will make the tattoo mark disappear. Another method has lately been suggested as the best ; a strong solution of tannin is put on the tattoo mark which is' then treated with a needle in the same way as in tattooing, and finally a strong solution of nitrate of silver is used. Tardieu also tried the following : acetic acid and fat, then potash, hydrochloric acid, and finally solution of potash. But the result of all these methods must always be that a scar however slightly visible will be left. '

TARLETON MURDERS


As D.A. Redmond observes (SHJ Vol. 12 No. 1) "No murders involving a Tarleton as either victim or criminal are recorded in the English or Scottish records from 1865 to 1890." A marginally possible identification occurs with the murders of Lord Leitrim and his clerk and driver in April 1875 at Milford in County Donegal. (Ref: MUSG)

## TETANUS

(L.: Gr.: Tetanos, tenein, to stretch) A disease due to bacillus, marked by painful tonic spasms of the muscles of the jaw and other parts. Bartholomew Sholto showed symptoms of tetanus (SIGN). Source: SIGN. See ALKALOID.

## TRANSPORTATION

The removal of offenders beyond seas to a penal colony. Transportation was common in England even for minor offences until it was finally abolished in 1868. Victor Trevor was transported to Australia in 1855 (GLOR).

## TREPOFF MURDER (1888? 1889?)

"From time to time I heard some vague account of his doings: of his summons to Odessa in the case of the Trepoff murder" — SCAN.

(The Dolsky murder (STUD) also happened at Odessa.) As Chris Redmond noted (SHJ Vol 7 No. 4), on Jan 24 1878, "General Trepoff, police prefect of St. Petersburg, was shot and wounded by a sixteen year old Nihilist named Vera Lassulic." Clearly, however, there is a problem of chronology.

## TRICHINOPOLY CIGAR

A cigar made from dark tobacco grown near Tiruchirapali in southern India. Enoch Drebber's killer smoked a Trichinopoly cigar. Holmes was acquainted with the ash of a Trichinopoly (RESI): 'To the trained eye there is much difference between the black ash of a Trichinopoly and the white fluff of bird's eye as there is between a cabbage and a potato" (SIGN).

## TYPEWRITER

Holmes was of the opinion that the typewriter has as much individuality as a man's handwriting and had thought of writing a monograph on the typewriter and its relation to the crime (IDEN). His analysis of the Sutherland case was determined by the characteristics of the typewriter (IDEN).

## UNKNOWN POISONS

In DYIN, Holmes' life is threatened by an unidentified bacterial poison sent to him by Culverton Smith in a special spring loaded box. Holmes, in discussing Smith's machinations with Watson, makes reference to the "Black Formosa Corruption" and Tapanuli Fever", fanciful names for unknown diseases.

Bacterial poisons were not unknown in the 19th Century, although instances of it are difficult to find. The most famous case was that of the Frenchman, Henri Gerard, who developed typhoid cultures and exposed the Parnotte family to the bacteria until one of the family succumbed. It is conceivable that the poison which killed young Victor Savage was a bacterial culture derived from cholera or typhoid, for Holmes' affected symptoms would suggest both as possibilities.

It will be recalled that Holmes used belladonna in his eyes in order to enhance his pretended delirium. According to Watson he was "well-up" in belladonna and it is a pity that Watson did not remember this for he would not have been duped so easily. Belladonna is so called because Italian women discovered that the pupils of their eyes became greatly expanded if a drop of the juice of this herb (otherwise known as Deadly Nightshade) were applied. Although belladonna is now rarely used for this purpose, the alkaloid which forms its chief constituent, atropine, is used in over thirty differing medical troubles, including Parkinson's disease.

Josiah Amberley, the retired colourman of Lewisham, sought to evade the justice of the courts by devouring a white pellet. According to Dr J.W. Sovine, this poison was either potassium cyanide or potassium ferrocyanide, both of which would bevailable to a maker of paints. This seems highly probable since cyanide is a fast acting poison which acts by interfering with the oxygen-carrying facility of the blood and paralysing the respiratory centre of the brain. Death from cyanide occurs within five minutes. (It was a favourite means of suicide among the Nazi war criminals.)

Anna, the Russian nihilist of GOLD, committed suicide by self-administering poison contained in a small phial. Maurice Campbell  suggests that this may have been Conine, otherwise known as hemlock, since this poison is almost without effect on the cerebrum, and causes death by respiratory paralysis.

Hemlock was used in ancient times to put criminals to death and is useful as an anodyne and sedative. Because of its effect, the user may remain conscious and lucid for some while before respiratory failure ensues. This would account for the period of time during which Anna was able to retain her faculties of thought and speech.

## VEHMGERICHT

A system of secret courts of revenge in medieval Germany. Alluded to in The Daily Telegraph article about the murder of Enoch Drebber (STUD). Source: STUD, Ch.6

## VIPER

(L. vipera-vivus, living; parere, to bring forth) The adder; any member of its genus (Vipers) or family (Viperidae), extended to some other snakes, as the pit-viperi, horned vipers, etc. Holmes had 'Vipers' as an entry in his index (SUSS); the box sent to Holmes by Calverton Smith had a poisoned spring 'like a viper's tooth' (DYIN), whilst Old Sherman threatened Watson with a 'Wiper' (SIGN). See Swamp Adder. Source: SIGN; SUSS; DYIN


## VITRIOL-THROWING

(Fr., L.L. vitriolum, of glass) Oil of vitriol: a hydrous sulphate of a metal, as blue, green and white vitriol: concentrated sulphuric acid. The throwing of sulphuric acid into someone's face so as to disfigure him or her. The blue carbuncle (BLUE) had been the subject of a vitriol-throwing. See also the vitriol-throwing at the conclusion of ILLU. The crime was remarkably common in Victorian times. Source: BLUE; ILLU. See ACID


## VOODOO

(W. African vodu, a spirit) Superstitions, beliefs and practices of African origin found also among the Negroes of the West Indies and southern United States, formerly including serpent-worship, human sacrifice and cannibalism, but now confined to sorcery. The mulatto (q.v.) cook practised voodooism, whilst Holmes consulted Eckermann's Voodooism And the Negroid Religions. Source: WIST


## WAINWRIGHT, Henry

Source: ILLU. Biographical details: Mentioned by Holmes when commenting on the fact that all great criminals have complex minds. Holmes claimed that "Wainwright was no mean artist" (ILLU). William S. Baring-Gould (*Sherlock Holmes: A Biography*) mistakenly assumes this to be Thomas Griffiths Wainewright (1794-1852). However, Watson's spelling was correct in this case. Henry Wainwright (executed in 1875) murdered his lover Harriet Lane in September 1874, dismembered her body with the aid of his accomplice, Alice Day, and kept the remains for a year in his warehouse in Vine Court. Lane's relatives had their suspicions aroused when, on visiting Wainwright, he told them that she had deserted him for another man and gone to Brighton to live. Stokes, his assistant, was also suspicious when, a year later, he was asked to load two heavy parcels into a four-wheeler. He looked inside one and discovered a woman's severed head, then gave chase and alerted two constables in the Borough. Wainwright was arrested on leaving the Hen and Chickens public house. An open grave was discovered when the Vine Court premises were subsequently searched, and further proof of murder was provided when it was revealed that Wainwright had purchased quantities of chloride of lime. Wainwright claimed his innocence to the last.

## WARBURTON, COLONEL

"... there were only two (cases) which I was the means of introducing to (Holmes') notice — that of Mr. Hatherley's thumb and that of Colonel Warburton's madness' - Dr. Watson, ENG

Colonel Sir Robert Warburton is listed in Who Was Who, 1897-1916. A contemporary of Holmes, Warburton wrote "Eighteen Years in the Khyber: 1879-1989." Warren Scheideman speculates (SHJ Vol 13 No. 2) that Watson may possibly have met Warburton. He was a friend of Edward VII, so may well have been linked with Holmes (Edward VII makes a thinly disguised appearance in SCAN). His involvement in the Khyber Pass events, Mr. Scheideman observes, may well have been regarded by the Foreign Office as a form of madness. (Also see Rolfe

Boswell, BSJ Vol No. 1 old series).

## WARD

A part of a lock of a special configuration to prevent its being turned by any except a particular key, or the part of the key of corresponding configuration. Holmes noted scratches on the ward on the inside of Blessington's strong box. Source: RESI.

## WOLFHOUND

A wolf-dog, especially of large size, as the Russian wolfhound (or Borzoi). Professor Presbury's wolf-hound objected to his master's simian behaviour. Source: CREE

## YEGGMAN

(U.S. sl. Possibly the name of an American safe-breaker) A burglar, esp. a burglar of safes. Holmes once referred to the case of 'Vanderbilt and the Yeggman'.Source: SUSS

## YELLOW FEVER

An acute disease occurring in tropical America and West Africa, caused by infection with a filter-passer conveyed to man by the bite of the mosquito. Aedes aegypti (Stegonyia fasciata), characterised by high fever, acute nephritis, jaundice and haemorrhages. Mr Hebron and his child died of this disease. Source: YELL; HOUN, Ch.3

## YEW

(O.E. iw, eow) Any tree of the genus Taxus - family Taxaceae, itself a division of the group coniferae; widely diffused over the northern parts of the world, with narrow lanceslate or linear leaves, esp. Taxus baccata (in Europe frequently planted in graveyards) which yields an elastic wood good for bows. A yew-alley led from Baskerville Hall to the summer house; here Charles Baskerville met his death. Source: HOUN

## ZINC

Holmes once traced a counterfeiter by means of the zinc and copper filings in the seam of his cuff. (SHOS)

# The Criminological Sherlock Holmes

## APPENDIX ONE:THE CRIMINOLOGICAL WORKS OF SHERLOCK HOLMES

Upon The Dating of Documents (pp. n.d.)
An exhaustive examination of handwriting, its variant forms, etc.
with a special section on forgery. The work also deals with paper
manufacture from the 16th Century onwards.

Upon Tattoo Marks (London, pp. 1878)
A guide to the varieties of tattooing both in the West and the
Occident, together with a chemical analysis of pigment used by
Japanese and Chinese artists.

Upon The Tracing of Footsteps
(London, pp. 1878. Reprinted by Magico Magazine, N.Y. 1983,
9pp.
A short introduction to the subject of footprints with some
remarks upon the uses of plaster of paris as a preserver of
impresses. A pioneering work which predates Hans Gross 's
Criminal Investigation.

Upon the Distinction Between The Ashes of The Various
Tobaccos. (London, pp.1879)
A highly lavish monograph listing 140 types of cigar, pipe and
cigarette tobaccos. The colour plates help the reader to make
distinctions between the varieties of leaf. The work contains a
chemical analysis of the ash of each listed tobacco.

The Book of Life
(The Fortnightly Magazine, March 1881)
An early magazine essay which discusses some of the premises of
Holmes' method. The work owes much to the theories of Darwin.
Part of the essay is quoted in STUD.

A Study of the Influence of a Trade upon the Form of a Hand (pp, 1886)
Holmes described this little brochure as "a curious little work" with "lithotypes of the hands of slaters, sailors, cork-cutters, compositors, weavers, and diamond polishers. This is a matter of great practical interest to the scientific detective - especially in cases of unclaimed bodies" (SIGN).
The work was rediscovered and reissued by Gilbert Forbes in The Police Journal, London, October - December 1946 and subsequently reprinted in the USA in The Journal of Criminal Law and Criminology, November - December 1947. (See G. Forbes' illuminating essay in BSJ 3, No. 4, 1948).

Malingering (London, pp.1888)
Holmes' own experiences as a protean actor suggested this monograph to him, as did his role in DYIN when his faked illness led to the arrest of Culverton Smith.

On The Variability of Human Ears
(The Anthropological Journal, September and October 1888)
These two short studies were later reprinted in The Strand Magazine for October and November 1893 and carry photographs of the ears of famous celebrities.

The Typewriter and its Relation to Crime (London, pp. 1890)
This short work carries a comprehensive set of illustrations showing the type faces of typewriters in use in the late 80's and 90's. There is also an analysis of defective key marks, plus a number of photographs showing the occupational spatulate markings exhibited by typists.

Secret Writings (Vols. 1 and 2) (London, pp.1896)

The Criminological Sherlock Holmes

A comprehensive guide to codes and ciphers.

## APPENDIX TWO: SHERLOCK HOLMES'
## UPON THE TRACING OF FOOTSTEPS

## CONTENTS

## FOREWORD

An observant man may learn much by an accurate and systematic
examination of the world. A momentary expression, a twitch of a
muscle, or a glance of an eye speaks volumes about a face, while
from a drop of water a logician can infer the possibility of an
Atlantic or Niagara without having seen or heard of one or the
other. So all life is a great chain, the nature of which is known
whenever we are shown a single link of it.
To the uninitiated reader these may seem to be preposterous
claims. But to the criminal investigator they form the bread and
butter of his existence. Like all other arts, the Science of
Deduction and Analysis is one which can only be acquired by

long and patient study, nor is life long enough to allow any mortal to attain the highest possible perfection in it. Let the inquirer begin by mastering elementary problems. Let him on meeting a fellow mortal learn at a glance to distinguish the history of the man and the trade or profession to which he belongs.

The exercise may seem puerile but it sharpens the faculties of observation and teaches one where to look and what to look for. By a man's fingernails, by his coat sleeve, by his boot, by his trouser knees, by the callosities of his forefinger and thumb, by his expression, by his shirt-cuffs, by each of these things a man's calling is plainly revealed.

I have endeavoured in this short monograph to concentrate on an aspect of the anatomy that has received scant attention among criminologists. To the student of natural history it is commonplace knowledge that the whole physical frame of a mammal may be constructed from a single foot impression. The foot is the key or lynch-pin to the body, for were it not to exist we would be altogether deprived of sustenance or the power to express ourselves. The foot is also the barometer of the personality, for in the way we walk are displayed all those minor idiosyncrasies and quirks which make us complete individuals. Therefore it is to the feet we should look when wishing to gauge the impression of a person, his limitations or powers, his strengths and weaknesses.

The study of foot impressions is therefore of vital interest to the serious investigator. It will provide not only a character brief but an indication of that person's whereabouts, his state of mind when passing from A to B, and the motive for adopting a particular route. If he is suspected of having participated in a crime, a foot impression may provide vital evidence. Therefore the preservation of that impression should be pursued with much diligence and in this regard a knowledge of the most up to date methods of creating casts can achieve remarkable results in the field.

## THE SUBJECT

A footprint may be defined as any impression made by the foot, by a boot, shoe, sock, or other type of apparel. The task of the criminal investigator is to isolate and identify that print which is his particular interest and deduce from it certain information about the owner. This task is complicated by the fact that when they do exist, prints are seldom complete or entire and may thus be rendered useless. Then there is the added complication of which print the investigator should localise. After a crime has taken place it is common for other people to gather round, thus obscuring the most important specimens. The interpretation and care of prints is therefore of paramount importance.

It is the writer's experience that prints are seldom preserved at the scene of the crime itself. Quite often the person or persons responsible seeks to obliterate any recognisable evidence of his presence and for this reason it is better to begin the investigation of prints at some distance from the crime.

The locality of the prints will vary greatly according to whether the crime takes place in town or country. In the former the choice may be limited to gardens or the margins of properties whilst in the latter the possibilities are much wider. But in both instances the prints of the criminal have the distinguishing factor of being clearly alien to the owners of the premises through which they pass. They will often be of the type which shows that the person was running at the time, i.e. a deep toe impression stretched at wide distances. In addition there may be other material evidence (stolen or lost articles) strewn along the route.

## THE MEASURING OF FOOTPRINTS

The measurements of footprints may vary considerably. There is in existence a calibrated scale used by the shoe trade from which the approximate size of the foot of an individual can be ascertained. Each foot is unique and indeed the size of the left foot may be quite different from that of the right even in the same set of prints.

## THE CREATION OF A PRINT

When the foot makes contact with the ground it is the back part of the heel that creates the initial impression and therefore it is more strongly impressed. The second deepest area of the print is that created by the toes, for it is there that the second fulcrum is created.

## THE HEEL

The movement of the heel is from above to downwards and from back to front. Owing to the heel giving slightly at the spot where it makes initial contact, the deepest part of the heel's impression occurs slightly in front of the place where it joined the ground. At this point therefore the soil is pushed forwards. When the sole comes down onto the ground directly in front of the heel it then pushes back the displaced sole. This effect creates the impression that the foot is smaller than it really is, and the investigator should take this into account.

## THE TRACE OF THE FOOTPRINT

The trace of a footprint may be defined as the whole impression of the person's walk, and by a careful analysis of the trace the peculiarities of that walk may be established.

# The Criminological Sherlock Holmes

(a) The Heel Line. By taking a photograph of a line of footprints and then joining a single line through the impressions of the heels the investigator will be able to establish whether the person has a well or poorly defined centre of gravity. In a normal or regular walk the feet are placed more or less perfectly one before the other, so the line of direction of the heels is the same as the line of march. Where the line of direction differs from the heel line, this indicates a swagger, drunken reel, or spreadeagled walk, for it suggests that the heels are not following in logical sequence.

(b) The Sole Line. Where the heel line is regular but the line of direction of the sole is not, we may deduce either that the toes are turned inwards or that they are turned outwards.

The Distance Between Steps. From the distance between steps it is possible to establish both the height of the person and his or her speed of travel. Both of these factors depend upon the size of the feet, e.g. if the distances between a smaller print are large and deeply impressed so that the toe and heel impressions are at a more acute angle than is normal, we may assume that a person was walking quickly. In a case in which the toe impresses alone remain and are separated at great distances, it is an indication that the person ran, for in this case the heels would not touch the ground.

*(Holmes' understanding of this type of impression led him to the deduction that Sir Henry Baskerville was running down the yew alley and not, as Dr. Mortimer suggested, "tiptoeing."— Editor.)*

## FURTHER OBSERVATIONS

Much may be gained by a study of anatomy and the development of the individual from youth to infirmity. The structure of the legs and the shape and condition of the joints (especially the joints of the pelvis) affects the positioning of the feet. For instance, the tendency to turn one foot out more than the other is common among young girls who have not attained puberty. The structure and condition of the foot also affects its impression. Flat-footed people walk with feet turned outwards because of the weakness of their tendons.

It must be remembered that the natural habit is to position the heels and soles in a straight plane because any variation towards the right or left means a diminution of locomotive power. But just because a footprint shows a tendency towards irregularity, we must not automatically assume lameness or infirmity. There may be exterior influences at work. The wearer of tight shoes will put his feet down to avoid discomfort, most probably at an inclined angle, while someone advancing up irregular or slippery ground will keep the feet straight to maintain the centre of gravity, as will the person bearing a heavy burden.

Again, a spreadeagled walk may mean a number of things. The oscillations in the walk may be due to obesity or even pregnancy, for in both cases the centre of gravity is pitched forwards of its customary position, so the soles must compensate by turning outwards in order to give the legs a firmer hold.

It is instructive to observe that when walking barefoot the natural condition is to place the feet squarely and in line. This is probably because the outside edge of the sole is less sensitive than the inside edge.

In the case of footprints that turn inwards, the possibilities are fewer. It is almost certainly due to some abnormality in the legs or spinal column. If either of the legs is twisted, the body is obliged to follow the direction of the sole of that foot so that an oscillation from side to side is produced. Persons suffering from spinal deformation normally produce irregular foot angles.

As regards the length of the step it may be stated that the taller the person the bigger the stride, except where infirmity or some muscular difficulty predominates. As a useful guide to the investigator I have observed that the average length of pace for a person walking unhurriedly approximates to 28 inches, while that of a brisk pace is on average about 32 inches. A fast sprint approximates to something like 40 inches.

It has also been observed that the pace shortens with age. The pace of a man of 40 years is about 30 ins while in a man of 30 it is usually about 33 ins.

Armed with the above information, the investigator should be able to determine the following information about the person he is pursuing:

(a) his age
(b) his speed and direction
(c) whether he suffers from any particular deformity of mind or body
(d) his weight
(e) his footwear

Once this information has been collated it becomes extremely difficult for him to deceive the investigator. For instance, in the case of a person who deliberately walks backwards, it will be observed that the stride is shorter, more uncertain and prone to irregularity, whilst the wearer of another's shoes can swiftly be detected since his mode of walking must compensate for the ill-fitting nature of the foot gear.

## CASTING THE PRINT

A cast is valuable because it provides a permanent replica of the original print and may be studied at leisure. Therefore it is to the investigator's advantage to look for the most reliable material in making the cast. Any material capable of changing from a plastic state to a solid condition may be used (even new breadcrumbs well kneaded together can serve as a cast) but they will, according to their particular qualities, give varying results. The ideal material is easy to apply, will not stick to the impression (the latter point being most important), and will have a fine smooth surface when rigid. The best material (best because of its cheapness and because it fits all the above criteria) which has so far emerged is plaster of Paris, a substance that has already proved its worth in dental and medical spheres. To obtain the best results with the material the user should observe the following conditions:
(a) The impression should be sealed at its margins to prevent leakage of the plaster. A strip of lead approximately 2 inches wide should suffice.
(b) Any remaining fluid left in the footprint should be drained off with the aid of a syringe.
(c) Impressions in dry dusty soil need hardening before exposure to the plaster. Cellulose acetate and acetone (approx 1/4 oz. to 10 oz.) in solution provide good results.
The plaster (which should be stored in air-tight tins) should be mixed into the water (not vice versa) with the aid of a spatula and stirred until a creamy consistency emerges. About 3 lbs. of plaster to 4 pints should suffice for one impression. When the mould is half full of the solution, it should be strengthened by the insertion of a piece of rag or hessian. The mould should be allowed to set for at least half an hour, and will remain fragile for a period of 24

hours. To achieve very rapid hardening, add to the solution a tablespoonful of common salt.

The investigator should at all times be prepared for failure in the operation, and since the impression may well be unique it is best to photograph the print first. A measure sunk into the ground by the side of the print will give an accurate record of its dimensions.

In the case of footprints found in snow, if the substance is compacted and hard the plaster may be poured straight in. But if it is soft and loose, treatment should be applied. The surface should be dusted first with French chalk and then sprayed several times with a solution. When this has hardened the plaster may be poured in. The method is perilous, however, and it is safer to take photographs.